Bridging the Gap

The amount of digital information that libraries need to manage effectively for the benefit of users is constantly increasing. This book discusses in detail how library administrators can better handle this growing abundance of information, as well as effective ways to allow library users easy access. Respected leaders in the field of librarianship explore various aspects of how librarians are meeting the challenges of delivering more digital information to a changing user base, including preservation demands, licensing agreements, digitizing and making available collections unique to specific libraries, and providing more personalized digital services to library users.

This book focuses on timely issues that impact how libraries are administered and viewed by both librarians and by users. This innovative book discusses practical ways to provide remote access and services to digital resources, support the preservation of digital resources, understand their library users who prefer the digital information format, and reshape the traditional library for better digital access. The book is carefully referenced and includes helpful illustrations.

The book is a valuable resource for senior and mid-level library administrators, including deans, directors, and department heads, of public, special and academic libraries.

This book was previously published as a special issue of the *Journal of Library Administration.*

Sul H. Lee is Peggy V. Helmerich Chair and professor of Library and Information Studies at the University of Oklahoma and Dean of University of Oklahoma Libraries. He is the editor of the *Journal of Library Administration* and serves regularly as consultant to library service providers, academic book vendors, publishers, and advises state and local governments on library affairs.

Bridging the Gap

Connecting Users to Digital Contents

Edited by Sul H. Lee

LONDON AND NEW YORK

First published 2010 in the USA and Canada
by Routledge
711 Third Avenue, New York, NY 10017

Simultaneously published in the UK
By Routledge
2 Park Square, Milton Park, Abingdon, Oxon, OX14 4RN

Routledge is an imprint of the Taylor & Francis Group, an informa business

© 2010 Edited by Sul H. Lee

Typeset in Times by Value Chain, India

All rights reserved. No part of this book may be reprinted or reproduced or utilised in any form or by any electronic, mechanical, or other means, now known or hereafter invented, including photocopying and recording, or in any information storage or retrieval system, without permission in writing from the publishers.

British Library Cataloguing in Publication Data
A catalogue record for this book is available from the British Library

ISBN10: 0-7890-3786-6 (hbk)
ISBN10: 0-7890-3787-4 (pbk)
ISBN13: 978-0-7890-3786-2 (hbk)
ISBN13: 978-0-7890-3787-9 (pbk)

CONTENTS

Notes on Contributors		vii
1	Introduction *Sul H. Lee*	1
2	Bridging the Gap: Wherever you are, the Library *Carla J. Stoffle, Kim Leeder, and Gabrielle Sykes-Casavant*	3
3	Responding to the Preservation Challenge: Portico, an Electronic Archiving Service *Eileen G. Fenton*	31
4	Assessing the Value and Impact of Digital Content *Brinley Franklin and Terry Plum*	41
5	All Hype or Real Change: Has the Digital Revolution Changed Scholarly Communication? *Barbara McFadden Allen*	59
6	A World Infinite and Accessible: Digital Ubiquity, the Adaptable Library, and the End of Information *Dennis Dillon*	69
7	Social, Intellectual, and Cultural Spaces: Creating Compelling Library Environments for the Digital Age *Barbara I. Dewey*	85
8	A Question of Access—Evolving Policies and Practices *Heather Joseph*	95
9	Funes and the Search Engine *Frank Menchaca*	107
	Index	121

Notes on Contributors

Barbara McFadden Allen is Director, Committee on Institutional Cooperation, Champaign, IL.

Gabrielle Sykes-Casavant is Special Assistant, Dean, University of Arizona Libraries.

Barbara I. Dewey, Dean of Libraries, University of Tennessee Libraries, Knoxville, TN.

Dennis Dillon is Associate Director for Research Services, University of Texas Libraries, University of Texas, TX.

Eileen G. Fenton is Executive Director, Portico, Princeton, NJ.

Brinley Franklin is Vice Provost, University of Connecticut Libraries, Storrs, CT.

Heather Joseph is Executive Director, The Scholarly Publishing and Academic Research Coalition (SPARC), Washington, DC.

Kim Leeder is Librarian, N. L. Terteling Library, Albertson College of Idaho, Caldwell, ID.

Frank Menchaca is Executive Vice President, Publishing, Gale, A port of Cengage Learning.

Terry Plum is Assistant Dean, Simmons Graduate School of Library and Information Science, Boston, MA.

Carla J. Stoffle, Dean, University of Arizona Libraries and Center for Creative Photography, Tucson, AZ.

Introduction

The papers delivered at the University of Oklahoma Libraries' 2007 annual conference in Oklahoma City, Oklahoma, addressed the challenge of connecting library users with the growing abundance of digital information now available. Libraries are now not only called upon to provide electronic resources, but increasingly are expected to deliver more services, meet new preservation demands, adhere to licensing agreements, and digitize and make available collections unique to their institutions. The ways librarians are responding to these issues are important to the library community, and we are fortunate to provide eight different approaches to the complex task of making digital resources more readily available to scholars, students, and researchers.

Carla J. Stoffle, dean of libraries and the Center for Creative Photography at the University of Arizona, and her associates Kim Leeder and Gabrielle Sykes-Casavant set the framework for the conference by noting that research libraries can no longer expect their patrons to come into the library proper for the information they may need. Libraries, she says, must provide their researchers with access from wherever the researcher may be, and should then be prepared to provide new services offering research access to information held by other institutions. This enhanced service approach has changed the way libraries are organized and staffed.

Preservation of library resources, paper or electronic, always has been one of the greatest challenges for research libraries. The advent and proliferation of electronic information has not lightened the burden in any way. The non-profit organization Portico has accepted the monumental task of preserving electronic scholarly journals for the future, and its executive director, Eileen Fenton, gives a history of its efforts to offer archival services to the library community for electronic scholarly journals.

Brinley Franklin, vice provost for University Libraries at the University of Connecticut, and his associate Terry Plum see the expanded availability and use of digital materials as a way to better understand the way libraries are used. He believes that evaluating user satisfaction, costs of digital resources, and identifying the users of digital information will give library administrations a perspective that was not previously available.

There is still much debate within the library community, however, on the value of digital information vis-à-vis traditional print materials. Barbara Allen, director of the Committee on Institutional Cooperation examines this debate and gives her insights on where academic libraries should be placing their collection development emphasis.

Dennis Dillon, associate director, University of Texas Libraries at Austin, offers a historical overview of collection development from the growth of traditional print collections in academic libraries to the concept of a network of digital information. He speculates that continued growth of electronic information resources may lead to the "end of information," or information so extensive that it can no longer be considered a collection.

The proliferation of digital resources also has led to a need for new environments within academic libraries. Barbara Dewey, dean of libraries at the University of Tennessee, lends her expertise on this subject by giving us an overview of what the University of Tennessee has done to make its traditional library more compatible with electronic resources and more useful and comfortable for the people who use them.

In the concluding two articles, both Heather Joseph, executive director for The Scholarly Publishing and Academic Resources Coalition and Frank Menchaca, executive vice president of Thomson Gale explore changes that digital publishing has brought to scholarly communications, the marketing of digital information, and the evaluation of scholarly publishing in place of traditional print scholarship.

While addressing very different aspects of digital information, these eight articles offer readers interesting and authoritative insights to the benefits and problems that electronic resources have brought to academic libraries. I am pleased to have the opportunity to present the work of these library community leaders to the wider audience that traditional publication still offers.

Sul H. Lee
Editor

Bridging the Gap: Wherever you are, the Library

Carla J. Stoffle
Kim Leeder
Gabrielle Sykes-Casavant

ABSTRACT. This paper argues that economics, not technology, is driving the need for fundamental changes in our universities and in our libraries. Success in the future will require libraries to deliberately adopt a "push out" philosophy in which the library extends outward to customers wherever they are and requires libraries to be customer-based, not place based or collection-driven. Libraries have and will continue to have a central role in higher education if we use our traditional strengths to change in ways that will fit, and add value to, our environment on campus and beyond.

KEYWORDS. Academic libraries, forecasting, change

An unspoken implication of the theme of this conference is that technology is driving libraries. Libraries must change because the technology is changing and because customers expect more, given the power of the technology they have at their desktop. Our customers enjoy the ease of searching on Google or shopping with Amazon and wonder why libraries can't deliver the same type of service. So, they turn to libraries as a second choice, a circumstance we must reverse lest we become irrelevant.

Before going on to discuss how our libraries need to change and how that change must address our approach to our work, the work itself, and how we organize ourselves to respond to our customers' expectations, it is important to emphasize the premise of this paper: that technology is not our primary driver. Google and Amazon notwithstanding, our cost structure and the nature of our cost increases—the economics of our libraries—are in fact driving the need for us to change and endangering our role on campus. Basically, our costs are increasing faster than any other sector of the higher education community, and our institutions, especially public ones, are receiving fewer funds or at least less new money than the yearly increased costs of the entire enterprise. Thus, our institutions have less money with which to support us. If we were receiving sufficient funding increases, we could maintain the library of the past (our legacy collections), operate the library of today, and create the library of the future in the mode expected by our customers. We could in fact meet almost everyone's expectations without drastic changes. However, we don't have these funds and so we must create the library of the future by a combination of actions that require a transformative vision and a transition plan.

In support of my argument that economics is driving our need for transformation in libraries, there are a variety of data and articles published about the sustainability of higher education when public funds and tuition limits conspire to reduce funding and/or ensure that funding increases are less than what is necessary to maintain the enterprise.[1] In this environment, institutions are driven by the necessity to reduce costs and increase productivity while adding value to our communities. Institutions are in fact being pushed to demonstrate their contribution to student learning and show how campus research benefits society at large. In this environment, technology, if utilized with a transformative vision, can enable the sustainability of our institutions and our libraries. In 2002, Alan Guskin and Mary Marcy, leaders of the three-year Project on the Future of Higher Education, addressed the economic problems in higher education and proposed a series of principles to be applied to transforming institutions rather than "muddling through" or cutting corners using a short-term strategy to deal with a long-term problem.[2] In response to this institutional view, Joseph M. Brewer, Sheril J. Hook, Janice Simmons-Welburn, and Karen Williams wrote an article applying to libraries the guidelines provided by the Project. Brewer et al. offered examples of ways libraries can move forward to transformation in a climate of constrained resources demanding greater accountability. They noted:

Libraries will accomplish this [transformation] by empowering individuals to work more independently, cooperating with each other to develop shared print repositories, working with vendors to receive shelf-ready books, increasing the amount of information available electronically, and reducing staff at service points. The transformation occurring in libraries will create new environments and resources for learning, scholarly communication, and information access.[3]

They also noted that libraries on the whole are already transitioning. In response to economic challenges, libraries have been streamlining processes, consolidating library units, and outsourcing work when possible; creating national networks and cooperatives to mitigate financial constraints; and reaching out to campus units to partner or cooperate on projects. For example, the University of Arizona Libraries have undertaken a number of projects to streamline work, the most recent of these was the Finding Information in a New Landscape (FINL) project, which reduced the cost of reference services.[4] Workflow redesign, as documented in the January 2007 Council on Library and Information Resources (CLIR) report, has also been the recent focus of grant-funded efforts at six academic libraries.[5] However, some of the efforts described by Brewer et al. are being done in a reactive mode without a purposeful vision of where these changes should lead us.

The purpose of this paper, based on our economic imperative and enabling technology, is to propose a context and vision for what we might be doing in the future and what we must change to achieve that vision. We propose to go beyond a description of discrete responses to economic pressures, no matter how creatively framed such responses may be. Rather, we advocate using these pressures in a manner that fundamentally changes what we do and how we function. We begin this discussion with a simple proposition, that success in the future will require libraries to deliberately adopt a "push out" philosophy—one in which the library extends outward to customers wherever they are—rather than wait for customers to come looking for the library or librarian either virtually or physically, or to even know they have an information need. A "push out" philosophy requires that we be customer-based, not place-based or collection-driven. This one change in our philosophy will transform library functions and staff roles. The resulting library might then have the following characteristics:

Librarians stimulate learning and research, not just support it when the student or scholar asks.
The library is a place for the production of knowledge.

Librarians are part of the creation process for new knowledge, new access tools, and new dissemination processes, including electronic publishing, that do not require mediation or instruction.

Librarians manage *campus* knowledge and information. We provide campus information services, not just access to library information, on a 24/7 basis.

We create physical and virtual learning environments for our campuses and are partners in the educational process. The library is an integral and interdependent part of the student's educational experience.

Collections are primarily in digital format. A smaller percentage of our budget is going to purchasing, processing, and managing commercial scholarly information, which reduces the cost of selecting, processing, housing and circulating print collections.

Our collection building is focused on special collections and unique resources while creating digital access to both.

All services offered by the library are available at the desktop and are customized for the individual user.

Librarians are an active part of an ongoing national system for maintaining and preserving information in all formats, through coordinated repositories, having less print on each campus.

Librarians are key players in a national system that monitors and influences national information policy, and we protect campus interests and access to information through national and local action as a basic part of what we do and are expected to do on campus.

The library organization is agile, flexible, and welcoming of change. The library is always looking to the future and expanding resources to be effective 3–5 years from now, rather than maximizing resources to support current services.

Some of our colleagues question whether our organizations, or even our profession, can make these changes and whether we have the skill or the will to do this.[6] Many of the things that are proposed here are, in fact, very hard to do. They run counter to many years of practice. However, the authors believe that libraries and librarians can transform, and that libraries have had, and will continue to have, a central role in higher education.

TRANSFORMING LIBRARIES

Many of the qualities we described above as characteristic of transformed libraries are already reflected in some of our daily operations.

However, we participate in most of these activities in addition to our business as usual, not instead of it. They are adjunct activities, not core activities. We have not made the leap to letting go of the library of the past (our legacy collections) and managing the library of the present to aggressively build the library of the future. Doing this involves:

Moving from cooperation to collaboration in our activities.
Only doing locally what must be done locally.
Focusing on the needs of our campus, which is not what libraries currently do.
Pushing all of our services to the desktop and embedding these and our collections into educational and research programs.
Rethinking collections, collection building, and the collection budget.
Redesigning our spaces as learning spaces.
Repurposing our library online catalogs and access tools.
Developing new performance and assessment measures.
Internalizing the concept of "planned abandonment," that is, encouraging the abandonment of programs and projects in decline to free up resources for innovative new projects.[7]
Creating new sources of revenue.
Utilizing our human resources differently.

This is not a formula for transformation, but these are the most essential directions we must pursue to address the challenges facing us. We must use technology not only to increase access but also to save money. Forget business as usual, it's time to charge into the future and make the changes our evolving environment demands.

1. From Cooperation to Collaboration

As Richard C. Insinga and Michael J. Werle note, "In order to do more with less, a company must focus its limited resources on those activities that are essential to its survival and must leverage activities that are peripheral. The result is a greater use of partnerships, collaborations, and simple buying to substitute for in-house capabilities."[8] First and most essential in the transformation process is for libraries to advance from cooperation to true collaboration in our activities. Mattessich, Murray-Close, and Monsey distinguish collaboration from cooperation in their book, *Collaboration: What Makes it Work,* and it is this distinction that we would like to make here. Cooperation describes informal relationships between organizations, relationships that do not imply any shared mission or authority. Collaborations, on the other hand, "bring previously separated organizations into a new structure with full commitment to a common mission."[9] This relationship requires a pooling of resources, a willingness to accept risks, and a shared authority fully given to the collaborative and not retained by any individual group.

Librarians have always been eager and willing to cooperate and share work when cooperation would provide a better service to the user, but the types of relationships existing between libraries have changed. "Thirty years ago most resource sharing took place between libraries, with a few formal organizations (library consortia) providing logistical support. Today there are hundreds, perhaps thousands, of organizations around the world facilitating resource sharing," notes Bernie Sloan.[10] This resource sharing is evident in vibrant library partnerships and consortia working to make possible interlibrary loan, cooperative cataloging, and group purchasing of digital databases and other costly items. Libraries share storage facilities and work together to create new resources and launch new forms of reference service. In addition, librarians have the Center for Research Libraries (CRL) to buy, house, and share expensive and important yet little-used materials so that individual libraries can avoid the cost of ownership—buying, processing, housing, and circulating such collections.

Yet while all of these are examples of cooperation that have improved services, some even saving money, none of these efforts reflect the qualities of true collaboration. These projects have not changed the way individual libraries function, nor have they changed the work of individual librarians. We are in no way committed to continuing these cooperatives should local conditions change. In the case of shared storage facilities, we have kept multiple copies of items in storage rather than rely on group ownership. Our collection activities continue as usual as long as we have the money to buy and store these items. Only when we do not have enough money do we depend on others. Business as usual continues under cooperative arrangements.

What we need in these changing times are truly collaborative projects that will save us staff time and resources. A true collaboration requires interdependence. This means we have to give up some aspects of our work to let others do them, while we agree to do other types of work and share the results. There is an element of risk in this type of relationship, and there must be a great amount of trust to believe that things will get done properly even if we aren't the ones doing them. We also must be receptive to the fact that collaboration will require a change in the way we do things; for some, job duties will change dramatically and we need to be ready to take on our new roles. For example, area studies selection and cataloging should be provided in a few centers around the country freeing up resources to catalog/provide metadata for unique campus resources. Or better yet, with the increasing global reach of the Online Computer Library Center (OCLC), relying on libraries in foreign countries and helping those libraries to build their electronic delivery mechanisms may be the most cost-effective and ultimately most accessible way of providing these materials.

If we can identify areas where collaboration can change the work we do locally, we can look at how to transform ourselves in those areas thereby shifting resources to new areas. For instance, we might point to interlibrary loan. Rather than simply trading documents, we could set up collaborations that not only impact service, but that change our collecting activities. We might resolve to collect in particular areas, while other libraries cover different areas. Doing so would mesh our collecting goals with those of our network libraries so that between all the libraries in our network we cover all print and online resources that we feel are important to our communities. We have made many attempts to do this, but have not yet really succeeded.

On a similar note, an increasing number of librarians, including Paul Gherman and Brinley Franklin, point to the need to reduce replication—regionally or even nationally—in library collections by truly collaborating on materials we store.[11] Changes in this manner not only increase the access we provide, but allow us to redirect collection dollars, space, and staff time in selecting, buying, processing, and circulating. Collaborative collection development projects, such as the grant-funded joint effort that the libraries of Colby, Bates, and Bowdoin colleges have undertaken, are examples of this type of effort.[12] This type of collaboration will change how our libraries function and are organized. Instead of remaining independent libraries, we become pieces of a larger whole, a whole that is vibrant, flexible, and ready for the future.

2. *Only Do Locally What Must Be Done Locally*

A second integral part of the transformed library will be a view toward sharing, outsourcing, or otherwise contracting out any work that can possibly be done outside the library. Our libraries should only do locally what must be done locally, or that which is most economically done locally or which will not be done by others. Furthermore, we should only do alone that for which we can't find partners in the work. Libraries may buy services through outsourcing, such as acquiring shelf-ready books. As Karen Calhoun noted in her report prepared for the Library of Congress, in actuality we should be moving to an environment where it is not necessary to create bibliographic records for, or process, any commercially available material on a local level.[13]

Of course, membership in library consortia or collaborations will imbue us with more buying and negotiating power on the consumer market, but most importantly collaborations could allow us to save staff time spent negotiating "deals" in each of our libraries. We probably don't take advantage of this because we can't agree on what we want to buy except at very gross levels. The idea is that we should not each have to do this function locally, nor should we have to keep track of each deal locally with local staff involved.

As an alternative to outsourcing, libraries should also look at creating collaborative partnerships to which we contribute funds in order to create a product or service that we need outside of the commercial sector. RAPID, an interlibrary loan service out of Colorado State University, has transformed interlibrary loan by delivering to the desktop in 24 to 48 hours copies of articles and book chapters. RAPID libraries, through their contributions to the development and maintenance of this product, not only provide better access but also reduce the cost of local interlibrary loan.[14] The Association for Research Libraries (ARL), LibQUAL +, Project SAILS (Standardized Assessment of Information Literacy Skills), and E-Metrics collaborations have improved the ability of the library community to assess local needs and measure instructional success, and, in the case of E-Metrics, contribute to our improved ability to measure the use of electronic materials in a cost-effective manner.[15] These projects represent activities that single libraries could not afford to undertake alone. Indeed, they should not have to when we all share the need for these tools. Collaborative projects have not only saved development costs, but ongoing staff costs have been avoided for some aspects of the work of these projects.

In the past, preservation was done at the local level. For the future, it is too expensive to be done in this way. The contribution of resources to Portico and LOCKSS are other examples of how libraries are working together to reduce the cost to each library trying to maintain staff and equipment to preserve access to digital materials. So far many libraries are engaging in these collectives voluntarily and not attempting to duplicate these services. But, when the local funding gets tight, will we let someone else do it, and/or will some of us go ahead and duplicate the capability with its attendant costs because we don't trust each other? Both options are counter to our long-term interests.

Institutional repository building is another area where we can choose to work together, share costs, and give up control to achieve better results. The infrastructure costs are staggering. There are examples of groups working together, such as the Texas Digital Repository, the Colorado Alliance, and a fledgling Greater Western Library Alliance program to coordinate and build digital assets shared among the GWLA libraries.[16] However, trying to create long-term commitments and operational understandings that benefit everyone equally is not possible at the moment because we are not going to find many projects where we equally receive the benefits. Thus, we have to be able to give up some self-interest and gain to make these shared repositories work.

In addition to looking at ways to collaborate with others of our own ilk, libraries need to consider partnerships with corporations and others in the private sector. We might look to partnerships with commercial organizations as another way of providing tools we need at reduced cost or cost avoidance savings. The Google digitization project is a prime example of such partnerships that may benefit the whole community. Making public domain materials easily available provides us with an opportunity to rethink our print collections and print repositories. The jury is still out on digitization plans for copyrighted materials and those plans may ultimately be derailed under the restrictive conditions for use now prescribed.

The ARL Scholar's Portal Project between seven libraries and Fretwell-Downing is another example of partnering on a major project in the commercial sector. The primary focus of the three-year effort was to build a federated search capability for commercial and non-commercial information products with relevancy and standardized results. Although the resulting product was not all what we hoped it would be, it did stimulate the marketplace to consider library needs and wishes for building better products. Furthermore, the staff of the various institutions learned a tremendous amount from each other about the difficulties of such an undertaking; this knowledge has been applied to other library developments. The ARL Scholar's Portal Project ultimately benefited the library community as a whole and hopefully saved the community costs as well. A vast amount of our daily work can be outsourced or shared with collaborative partners, lightening the load of every individual library. This frees us to focus on the unique needs of our campus communities.

What needs to be done locally is managing and building access to local resources, those owned by the library and those owned by other campus units. This leads us nicely to our next section.

3. Focus on the Needs of Our Campus

The third thing libraries must do to transform themselves is put aside the concept of "what we do" especially as it applies to managing libraries and commercial scholarly information. We must develop a focus on the campus customer and needs of the campus. We must aggressively seek out ways to work and connect with other groups or departments, whether by providing services, applying our expertise, or drawing together and helping to manage campus resources. Librarians must be out on the campus identifying new opportunities for adding value to instruction and research activities or even helping service units better serve the needs of students. This will require the building of collaborations on campus, and is an outgrowth of only doing locally what is necessary to do locally.

Libraries should partner with other campus organizations to volunteer the unique skills of librarians in cross-campus initiatives. For example, a number of libraries are working with faculty to create new online journals and databases or to digitize back files of print materials, including journals, to make them available. Examples of this at the University of Arizona are two new journals, the *Journal of Insect Science* and the *Journal of Political Ecology*, and two open access archives for the *Journal of Rangelands Management* and *Radiocarbon*. We serve as an electronic archival site for the *Journal of Evolutionary Ecology Research*; as such, other libraries are ensured continued access to this faculty-created journal. At Arizona, we have also worked with our faculty to create public and campus educational materials having to do with rangelands management. These materials have ended up in the AgNIC (Agricultural National Information Network) database. We have contributed to the GROW (Geotechnical, Rock & Water) digital library, a civil engineering database created by campus constituencies to provide students and professionals open access to interactive digital learning objects in those fields. (For an overview of digital outreach projects at the University of Arizona Libraries, see Appendix A.)

While not unique among libraries, our librarians at Arizona have also identified distinctive campus collections and provided cataloging to make these fugitive non-library collections more accessible locally and nationally. Librarians have also joined with the University Teaching

Center to participate in faculty development activities and added other campus libraries to our federated searching capability. We have joint digital collection building projects with units like the UA Herbarium to digitize photographs from the 1920s and 1930s and have added a scanning capability so that we can scan materials as a service to other campus units. For example, we scanned and organized the formerly all paper human subjects research forms and, for our Department of Linguistics, we digitized a microfilm collection of a native language in Northern California. We are also working on a project to digitize the meeting minutes and attachments of our Faculty Senate thereby making these more accessible and freeing up physical space on campus. We have also partnered with our campus career services unit to make available *Résumé Builder*, a management service that allows students to produce high quality, discipline-specific résumés both within the libraries and at the career services center where students can receive individual assistance if needed. We are adding more instructional software such as MathWorks and ChemOffice to standard software available from the library. We have also proposed that the libraries take over the licensing of instructional software where multiple campus units are involved, saving students and campus departments money. We have provided staff to serve on the group that developed the campus Web presence and we are the Digital Millennium Copyright Act (DMCA) representative for the campus. Our latest project is one that will bring together under one umbrella Web page the digital instructional materials on campus that might be of use to K–12 teachers. This project will provide suggestions for campus Web sites and will provide training for teachers, librarians, and extension agents throughout the state in how to find and use these digital instructional materials.

As we look to what else we should be doing, we believe that our information desks should expand coverage to incorporate general campus information, rather than focusing solely on library information. We are looking at the upcoming campus need to manage databases and data sets that result from National Institutes of Health (NIH) funded research. We are looking at campus telephone services that are available only 40 hours per week to determine if our extended hours staff could be of help. We are also reviewing other duplicative information desks and reviewing campus Web pages and services to see if we might make a contribution. A focus on the needs of the campus is ultimately about a new view of the library's role on campus with an openness to view campus information needs and/or gaps as places where the libraries should make a contribution.

4. Provide All Services to the Desktop

The fourth thing libraries need to do, as part of our transformation is to provide services to the desktop, provide individual customization, and embed our library services and resources in the activities of our customers to the greatest extent possible. Reference services should be available online in e-mail and chat forms; interlibrary loan requests should be submitted and documents delivered virtually; and course reserves should be available online through a campus course management system rather than a stand-alone library system. The more information we can provide in digital format, the better we will please the majority of our customers. We must place an emphasis on creating tools and exploring ways to stimulate research, particularly online.

Library services provided to the desktop should also include services for use by faculty in their classes. Developing such options requires talking to faculty to learn their goals and designing instructional programs that will meet their needs. To help faculty be more effective and enable their students to increase information fluency, libraries should be working with faculty on well-designed assignments that incorporate information resources, new technologies, and active learning. Working with faculty, and not independently of faculty, we should be developing course management systems that integrate information resources easily and embed the librarian as part of the course. Victoria Matthew and Ann Schroeder have offered their experiences with the development, implementation, evaluation, and success of an embedded librarian program at the Community College of Vermont.[17] Creating reusable digital instruction objects and modules that can be used in classes as needed and referred to when students are actually working on a project should be high priorities for librarians. We should be pushing out the library services and resources, stimulating use for learning and research. Students and faculty should not have to come to the library and should not even have to seek the "library" online to find the library.

Some libraries, including Arizona State University Polytechnic Library and the Biosciences and Engineering Libraries at the University of California–Berkeley, are pushing subject-specific acquisitions updates to users who subscribe to library RSS feeds. In addition to pushing acquisition information to users, RSS is also being used to meet students in their personal blog space. An exploratory study at the Georgia Tech Library monitored the personal blogs of forty students who had identified Georgia Institute of Technology as their academic institution. By marking the incoming RSS feeds with keyword alerts (e.g., library, paper, reserve, test, etc.) the librarian leading this project was able to post on the student blog and offer reference assistance, marketing of library services, and explanations from the library's perspective.[18] In these ways, technology is further enabling libraries to meet our users where they are, regardless of their physical or virtual location.

5. Rethinking Collections, Collection Building, and the Collection Budget

When asked why he robbed banks, Willy Sutton is purported to have said, "Because that's where the money is." The largest portion of money to build our transformed libraries will have to come from the collections budgets and the staff who select, buy, process, shelve and circulate our print collections. This is where the money is in our libraries. Our current emphasis on our primary function of buying or leasing commercial information is unsustainable. According to David Lewis, it is more or less inevitable that increasing amounts of information desired by our customers will not be materials purchased by our libraries.[19] In this environment it will be nearly impossible to convince campus administrators to continue funding library collections budgets and their yearly inflation, let alone the costs of staff to select, buy, process, and shelve print materials for a smaller and smaller number of uses. This will not only force us to expend larger proportions of our budgets for digital materials, but will also necessitate that we redirect money and people to creating new information sources and managing types of information for which we have had no responsibility in the past. One example of this is data sets. We may either do this locally or in consortium, but we must be seen as expanding the information available rather than managing budgets that purchase less information each year. In addition, "just-in-case" buying and item-by-item selection will have to be things of the past. Other than through crafting approval plans, it may be that most of our monographic buying will be directed by user requests. It is important that we take the necessary actions now before we lose the ability to keep and manage these funds.

As far as physical collections go, we should focus on the collections we have built or are building that are unique—our special collections, including materials that are rare or generally unavailable. We will use the new collection analysis tools to determine which collections, or items, these are. Then we will need to find ways to make these more accessible, such as by digitizing them or providing detailed online exhibits.

Legacy collections have historically been a core focus in libraries, and many librarians are, understandably, protective of them. These massive print collections have taken tremendous time and energy and care to create, and watching them become extinct—as if they were dinosaurs facing an advancing ice age—can be a terrible thing when we are unsure of what is to follow. Yet however terrible it may be, we must face the fact that our future is digital and our continued dedication to legacy collections will only hurt us in the upcoming years. The resources that we currently devote to these collections, including money, staff time, and space would be better directed to supporting cutting-edge new digital projects or the establishment of open access repositories and journals that will better serve us and our customers in the foreseeable future.

6. *Redesigning Library Spaces*

Another point we want to mention as an integral part of the transformed library is *space*. In the past we dedicated our spaces to our physical collections, but these spaces are being increasingly replaced with group work areas and computer workstations. This is a positive movement, necessitated by cultural change, that acknowledges the growing importance of digital resources and group work, and that will ensure the library's integrated position within its college or university. However, rather than simply pulling out shelves and installing computers to meet short-term demands, libraries need to make sure they are making conscious and deliberate choices in redesigning their spaces. Print collections will be removed in greater quantities over the upcoming years, and libraries need to be prepared to replace them with areas designed not just for machines but also for people, and more specifically for collaborative learning. Library designer Geoffrey T. Freeman describes this ideal vision: "A student can go to this place called the 'library' and see it as a logical extension of the classroom. It is a place to access and explore with fellow students information in a variety of formats, analyze the information in group discussion, and produce a publication or a presentation for the next day's seminar."[20]

With all of the convenience offered by digital materials, people no longer *need* to come to the library. But they will choose to for research, study, and even for socializing as long as the library offers a learning environment that provides them with a variety of welcoming spaces: quiet reading areas, bustling cafés, group study rooms of varying sizes, presentation practice rooms, and so on. Stephen R. Acker and Michael D. Miller advise,

"It might be tempting to build more traditional group study rooms with fixed walls. ... Open office systems and movable walls with easy access to whiteboards, presentation technology, power, and wireless networking should do better over time at adapting to changing technology and learning styles."[21] Libraries must assess the needs and desires of their communities and thoughtfully redesign space according to their findings. Libraries must also maintain an open-minded imagining of how those needs may change.

7. Repurposing Library Catalogs

In a study commissioned by the Library of Congress, Karen Calhoun concludes: "The existing local catalog's market position has eroded to the point where there is real concern for its ability to weather the competition for the information seeker's attention."[22] It is already clear that most of our users do not start an information search with our online catalogs. Indeed, the OCLC *Perceptions of Libraries and Information Resources* clearly documents this reality.[23] Many of our catalogs are confusing and do not facilitate identification and easy linking to the electronic resources that we own, let alone provide access to other unique campus collections or the conveniences of individual customization offered by a Google or Amazon search.

Studies by Karen Markey, The Indiana University Task Force on the Future of Cataloging, the University of California Bibliographic Services Task Force, and Karen Calhoun's LC report, propose changes to local catalogs to make them more effective and thereby more competitive access tools.[24] These recommendations will require a great deal of new skills and retooling, and it is not clear that the library community has yet embraced these. Needless to say, it is critical that we find ways to make our resources visible to our users, whether they use the local catalog or not, if we are to ensure that wherever they start their search and "wherever you are, the library."

At the University of Arizona, we have approached this issue through a project called "Unbundling the Catalog." As described by Marda Johnson:

> the objective for the *Unbundling the Catalog Project* is to reorganize the component parts of the online catalog [beginning with the descriptive and holdings metadata] to ensure that all information resources provided by the University Library are efficiently accessible by our authorized customers/stakeholders *regardless* of where they begin their search process. This project will:

Define with whom (vendors) we should work to expose our holdings [clearly inform our users what they can access freely and through whom];

Evaluate and determine upon which platform(s) we should keep our descriptive metadata, e.g., Google, Yahoo, MSN, OCLC;

Evaluate and determine the best methods for storing and providing our expanding metadata for preservation and access;

Determine best methods for providing free online public access to our information resources to our authorized customers;

Ensure that any new workflows become functional, ongoing, sustainable work utilizing limited resources.[25]

The bottom line for all of us is that we need to find ways to expose our collections wherever people start their search and link related collections on campus and locally through federated searches. We also need local catalogs that always end in an action available to the user and that are designed to reach out to the user. Other than this, our emphasis needs to be on making local unique collections visible rather than devoting time and effort to cataloging commercially available materials. Above all, our catalogs need to be re-imagined to provide the ease of use, personalization, and user-friendliness that have caused our customers to flock to Amazon and Google.

8. *Develop New Performance and Assessment Measures*

Let us move now into discussing how libraries might measure their success under this new system, and how we might support it. We believe that the more we pursue the types of work described above, the more our assessment of libraries will have to change. In the old model, we looked at how large the budget was and how many holdings the library had in order to judge whether it was a great library or not. This model must be turned inside out. There is increasing demand for libraries to demonstrate outcomes and impacts in areas of importance to their institutions, and increasing pressure to maximize the use of their limited resources through benchmarking that will result in cost savings and reallocation of funds. If what we count determines what we do, we will need to find different things to measure. As we discussed our need to serve our campus goals and not just the goals of the library, so too is it essential that we assess ourselves on the value we add to organizationally identified outcomes. These outcomes include how the library makes a difference to its constituents, how it compares to similar institutions, and what it contributes to the education of students.

One way to get away from the descriptive data of collection size, budget, staffing, and door counts, is to move into using new tools to measure our success. The ARL New Measures Initiative seeks to respond to this need by establishing new data gathering and statistical analysis tools to measure the success of our libraries. Some of the tools being developed by the ARL New Measures Initiative include LibQUAL +, DigiQUAL, and MINES (Measuring the Impact of Networked Electronic Services) for Libraries. These tools offer a more holistic assessment of the physical and digital libraries, which includes role, character, and impact. Libraries can also use the E-Metrics project to standardize use data from vendors and can gather data from Project SAILS, headquartered at Kent State University, which offers standardized assessment of student information literacy based on ACRL standards. We need tools that assess our service orientation, our electronic resource access, and the ability to streamline our operations and provide seamless access to our library customers. As we change the work that we do, we must continue to find new statistical ways to assess the progress that we're making across campus and across libraries overall.

9. *Internalize the Concept of "Planned Abandonment"*

Peter Drucker describes the management concept of "planned abandonment" this way: "Every three years, every organization—not just business—should sit down and look at every product and every service and every policy and say, 'If we didn't do this already, knowing what we now do, would we go and do it?' And if the answer is no, don't make another study."[26] The primary purpose of this perspective is to eliminate projects or programs before they go into decline with the purpose of freeing up those resources—staff, financial, and otherwise—to pursue new, more innovative projects that will move the organization forward. This concept applies to all organizations, and is greatly relevant to libraries in general, particularly at this moment in time.

Planned abandonment requires us to recognize programs and services that are not as successful as they should be, and to make a conscious choice to give them up before finances force us to eliminate them. This is a difficult challenge for librarians, as we typically hesitate to end a service even if there is one person in our entire community who uses it. We must acknowledge that programs and services used by only one person, or a small number of people, are draining away resources that could be used to create new, improved services that would be more successful and benefit larger numbers of people. Giving up the less successful services allows for a reallocation of funding and staff time into services that would better meet the needs of our communities, and use funding more efficiently.

10. Create New Resources for Revenue

The new economic environment will require libraries to find new resources for funding the library. Brinley Franklin recently surveyed ARL Libraries and discovered that, on average, 85 percent of the library's revenue is generated from tuition and state funds.[27] We will have to rely less on institutional general fund support and become more entrepreneurial.[28] This will mean developing business plans and assessing the opportunity for a meaningful return on investment.

Some libraries have already turned to students and student fees. Others are charging for some services on a cost recovery basis, expanding the traditional photocopy and printing operations to include supplies and creating specialized materials like posters. Many others are moving aggressively to create strong fundraising and grant programs by building fundraising and grant-writing activities into the job descriptions of every librarian as well as creating a development office with high-level staffing.

As an additional option to increase the revenue stream, many libraries across the country have begun hosting coffee shops, fast food, and other dining options inside their doors, or at least right outside. The success of these options in bookstores reflects a viability that libraries can and should cash in on as well. In addition to food services, gift shops selling library-logo office supplies and other gear are appearing in libraries as another way to financially support library operations and acquisitions. Providing scanning services and building rights and reproduction services out of special collections are other ways libraries can supplement their budgets. The bottom line is that streamlining and effective management, coupled with institutional support, are not enough to sustain the transformed library. Finding new revenues within our value system to expand and support our work is necessary.

11. Utilize Our Human Resources Differently

It is important as we undertake the transformation of our libraries that we make the most effective use of our human resources possible. We will need people working at the top of their skill levels who are flexible, risk-takers, and continuous learners. We must also have people who share the philosophy of empowering customers to be self-sufficient to the greatest extent possible. Disintermediating work must be a goal, and there must be constant assessment of the skills needed to do the work. It is very likely that the management of in-house library services—information desks, reserves, interlibrary loan, etc.—and physical facilities—will be in the hands of professional staff members who are not librarians. Likewise, systems support, in-house processing, and business functions will require professionals who may or may not be librarians.

Librarians will be training; designing programs, services, and learning environments; building instructional programs and new access systems; assessing and evaluating programs and services; assigning metadata; working out on campus; and creating and managing collaborations. Librarians will be identifying and expanding our unique special collections regardless of format and will be determining ways to make all collections and services more accessible. It is probable that these changes will alter our organizational structures and perhaps impact the educational backgrounds of our staff. However, it is the special knowledge base and philosophy of librarianship that will drive: "wherever you are, the library."

CONCLUSION

The times are changing and the financial environment—which shows no sign of reversing—is going to ensure that libraries change whether we like it or not. Our choice is between continuing to try to muddle through, allowing our services and resources to degrade and our staff numbers to dwindle, and embracing the times and responding with a collective energy to turn these changes to our benefit. Changing with the times will require new skills, a wider variety of professionals, full utilization of all staff talents, appreciation for diverse perspectives, and a critical review of management and compensation systems. Overall it requires a re-envisioning of the role of the library on campus and within the information field. We must be ready and willing to make dramatic changes in the way we do business.

The digital revolution will work in our favor if we take advantage of it to reinvigorate our libraries. Geoffrey T. Freeman observes, "Rather than threatening the traditional concept of the library, the integration of new information technology has actually become the catalyst that transforms the library into a more vital and critical intellectual center of life at colleges and universities today."[29] If we can give up our traditional understandings of library work and collaborate with others to take action, we will see a transformation that makes our work more efficient and increases our value to the higher educational institutions we serve.

All in all, this is a time of great opportunity for libraries if we are willing to undergo transformation to meet the challenges and demands we face. The first step is for us to begin to see these challenges in terms of opportunity, not threat. If we are afraid, we will be frozen in place; we need to shed our fears and welcome change not only as inevitable but as a healthy process. We cannot avoid change, we can only meet it and find ways to be more agile and creative with the resources we have. It is important above all that we learn to anticipate, welcome, and exploit change. The qualities described in this paper as those of a transformed library are just the beginning of what is sure to be the long-term evolution in our field. Yet these steps will guide us forward to a new kind of librarianship in which we will be well positioned to embrace the unpredictable twists and turns coming up on the pathway of our future.

NOTES

1. Robert C. Dickeson, *Frequently Asked Questions About College Costs*, issue paper prepared at the request of the U.S. Department of Education, 2006; Larry R. Faulkner, "Public Universities will Survive. Can Public Higher Education?" (Clair Maple Memorial address, Seminars on Academic Computing, Snowmass, CO, August 4, 2003); Postsecondary Education Opportunity, "State Tax Fund Appropriations for Higher Education FY1961 to FY2005," *Postsecondary Education Opportunity* 151 (2005): 1–20.

2. Alan E. Guskin and Mary B. Marcy. "Dealing with the Future Now," *Change* 35, no. 4 (2004): 10–21.

3. Joseph M. Brewer, Sheril J. Hook, Janice Simmons-Welburn, and Karen Williams, "Libraries Dealing with the Future Now," *ARL Report* 234 (2004): 8.

4. John N. Berry III, "Arizona's New Model," *Library Journal* 127, no. 18 (2002); Joseph R. Diaz and Chestalene Pintozzi, "Helping teams work: Lessons learned from the University of Arizona Library reorganization," *Library Administration & Management* 13, no. 1 (1999); Marianne Bracke et al., "Finding Information in a New Landscape: Developing new service and staffing models for mediated information services," *College and Research Libraries* 68 (forthcoming).

5. Marilyn Mitchell, ed., "Library Workflow Redesign: Concepts and Results," Pages 1–9 in *Library Workflow Redesign: Six Case Studies*, Washington, DC: Council on Library and Information Resources, 2007.

6. Jerry D. Campbell, "Changing a Cultural Icon: The Academic Library as a Virtual Destination," *Educause Review* 41, no. 1 (2006): 16–30; James G. Neal, "Raised by Wolves," *Library Journal* 131, no. 3 (2006): 42–44.

7. Peter F. Drucker and Peter M. Senge, *Leading in a Time of Change: What It Will Take to Lead Tomorrow, Viewer's Workbook* (New York, NY: Jossey-Bass, 2001).

8. Richard C. Insinga and Michael J. Werle, "Linking Outsourcing to Business Strategy," *The Academy of Management Executive* 14, no. 4 (2000): 58.

9. Paul W. Mattessich, Marta Murray-Close, and Barbara R. Monsey, *Collaboration: What Makes it Work*, 2nd ed. (St. Paul, MN: Amherst H. Wilder Foundation, 2001), 60.

10. Bernie Sloan, "Evolution Takes a Leap," *Netconnect*, April 2005: 2.

11. Paul Gherman, Duane Webster, and Brinley Franklin, "The Director's Panel" (presentation, Living the Future 6 Conference, Tucson, AZ, April 6–8, 2006).

12. Bowdoin College, "Broader Universe Awaits Libraries at Colby, Bates, and Bowdoin," *Bowdoin Campus News*, January 3, 2007, http://www.bowdoin.edu/news/archives/1bowdoincampus/003684.shtml.

13. Karen Calhoun, "The Changing Nature of the Catalog and Its Integration with Other Discovery Tools," (Prepared for the Library of Congress), March 17, 2006: http://www.loc.gov/catdir/calhoun-report-final.pdf.

14. Linda Dols, "Interlibrary Loan Journal Article Cost Analysis" (Document Delivery Team, University of Arizona, 2007), 1.

15. For additional information about ARL initiatives visit, *Association of Research Libraries New Measures and Assessment Initiatives*, http://www.arl.org/stats/initiatives/index.shtml.

16. For additional information about these collaboratives visit the *Texas Digital Repository*, http://dspace.lib.utexas.edu/; the *Colorado Alliance*, http://www.coalliance.org/; the *Greater Western Library Alliance*, http://www.gwla.org/.

17. Victoria Matthew and Ann Schroeder, "The Embedded Librarian Program," *Educause Quarterly*, 4, (2006).

18. Brian S. Matthews, "Intuitive Revelations: The Ubiquitous Reference Model" (preliminary findings, Georgia Tech Library, Atlanta, 2006).

19. David W. Lewis, "Reflections on the Future of Library Collections," (presentation, Living the Future 6 Conference, Tucson, AZ, April 6–8, 2006).

20. Geoffrey T. Freeman, "The Library as Place: Changes in Learning Patterns, Collections, Technology, and Use," Pages 1–9 in *Libraries as Place: Rethinking Roles, Rethinking Space,* Washington, DC: Council on Library and Information Resources, 2005: 4.

21. Stephen R. Acker and Michael D. Miller, "Campus Learning Spaces: Investing in How Students Learn," *Educause Research Bulletin* 8 (2005): 5.

22. Karen Calhoun, "The Changing Nature of the Catalog and Its Integration with Other Discovery Tools," (Prepared for the Library of Congress), March 17, 2006: 10, http://www.loc.gov/catdir/calhoun-report-final.pdf.

23. Cathy De Rosa, *Perceptions of Libraries and Information Resources: A Report to the OCLC Membership* (Dublin, OH: OCLC Online Computer Library Center, 2005).

24. Markey, Karen. "The Online Library Catalog: Paradise Lost and Paradise Regained?" *D-Lib Magazine* 13, no. 1/2 (2007), http://www.dlib.org/dlib/january07/markey/01markey.html; Indiana University, "A White Paper on the Future of Cataloging at Indiana University," January 2006, http://www.iub.edu/~libtserv/pub/Future_of_Cataloging_White_Paper.pdf; University of California Libraries, "Rethinking How We Provide Bibliographic Services for the University of California," December 2005. http://libraries.universityofcalifornia.edu/sopag/BSTF/Final.pdf.

25. Marda Johnson, "Unbundling the Catalog" (project team report, University of Arizona Libraries, 2007), 1.

26. Drucker and Senge, *Leading in a Time of Change*, 34.

27. Brinley Franklin, e-mail message to ARL Director's discussion list, unpublished data, December 22, 2006.

28. James G. Neal, "The Research and Development Imperative in the Academic Library: Path to the Future," *portal: Libraries and the Academy* 6, no. 1 (2006).

29. Freeman, "The Library as Place," 2.

BIBLIOGRAPHY

Acker, Stephen R., and Michael D. Miller. "Campus Learning Spaces: Investing in How Students Learn." *Educause Research Bulletin* 8 (2005): 1–11.

Berry, John N. III. "Arizona's New Model." *Library Journal* 127, no. 18 (2002): 40–43.

Bowdoin College. "Broader Universe Awaits Libraries at Colby, Bates, and Bowdoin." *Bowdoin Campus News*, January 3, 2007. http://www.bowdoin.edu/news/archives/1bowdoincampus/003684.shtml.

Bracke, Marianne, Michael Brewer, Robyn Huff-Eibl, Daniel R. Lee, Robert Mitchell, and Michael Ray. "Finding Information in a New Landscape: Developing new service and staffing models for mediated information services." *College and Research Libraries* 68 (forthcoming).

Brewer, Joseph M., Sheril J. Hook, Janice Simmons-Welburn, and Karen Williams. "Libraries Dealing with the Future Now." *ARL Report* 234 (2004): 1–9.

Calhoun, Karen. "The Changing Nature of the Catalog and Its Integration with Other Discovery Tools." Prepared for the Library of Congress, March 17, 2006. http://www.loc.gov/catdir/calhoun-report-final.pdf.

Campbell, Jerry D. "Changing a Cultural Icon: The Academic Library as a Virtual Destination." *Educause Review* 41, no. 1 (2006): 16–30.

De Rosa, Cathy. *Perceptions of Libraries and Information Resources: A Report to the OCLC Membership*. Dublin, OH: OCLC Online Computer Library Center, 2005.

Diaz, Joseph R., and Chestalene Pintozzi. "Helping teams work: Lessons learned from the University of Arizona Library reorganization." *Library Administration & Management* 13, no. 1 (1999): 27–36.

Dickeson, Robert C. *See* U.S. Department of Education.

Dols, Linda. "Interlibrary Loan Journal Article Cost Analysis." Document Delivery Team, University of Arizona Libraries, 2007.

Drucker, Peter F., and Peter M. Senge. *Leading in a Time of Change: What It Will Take to Lead Tomorrow, Viewer's Workbook*. New York: Jossey-Bass, 2001.

Faulkner, Larry R. "Public Universities will Survive. Can Public Higher Education?" Clair Maple Memorial address, Seminars on Academic Computing, Snowmass, CO, August 4, 2003.

Freeman, Geoffrey T. "The Library as Place: Changes in Learning Patterns, Collections, Technology, and Use." In *Libraries as Place: Rethinking Roles, Rethinking Space*, 1–9. Washington, DC: Council on Library and Information Resources, 2005.

Gherman, Paul, Duane Webster, and Brinley Franklin. "The Director's Panel." Presented at the Living the Future 6 Conference, Tucson, AZ, April 6–8, 2006.

Guskin, Alan E., and Mary B. Marcy. "Dealing with the Future Now." *Change* 35, no. 4 (2004): 10–21.

Indiana University. "A White Paper on the Future of Cataloging at Indiana University." January 15, 2006. http://www.iub.edu/~libtserv/pub/Future_of_Cataloging_White_Paper.pdf.

Insinga, Richard C., and Michael J. Werle. "Linking Outsourcing to Business Strategy." *The Academy of Management Executive* 14, no. 4 (2000): 58–70.

Johnson, Marda. "Unbundling the Catalog." Project team report, University of Arizona Libraries, 2007.

Lewis, David W. "Reflections on the Future of Library Collections." Presented at the Living the Future 6 Conference, Tucson, AZ, April 6–8, 2006.

Markey, Karen. "The Online Library Catalog: Paradise Lost and Paradise Regained?" *D-Lib Magazine* 13, no. 1/2 (2007). http://www.dlib.org/dlib/january07/markey/01markey.html.

Mattessich, Paul W., Marta Murray-Close, and Barbara R. Monsey. *Collaboration: What Makes it Work. 2nd ed.* St. Paul, MN: Amherst H. Wilder Foundation, 2001.

Matthew, Victoria and Ann Schroeder. "The Embedded Librarian Program." *Educause Quarterly* 4, (2006): 61–65.

Matthews, Brian S. "Intuitive Revelations: The Ubiquitous Reference Model." Preliminary findings, Georgia Tech Library, Atlanta, March 13, 2006.

Mitchell, Marilyn, ed. *Library Workflow Redesign: Six Case Studies.* Washington, DC: Council on Library and Information Resources, 2007.

Neal, James G. "Raised by Wolves." *Library Journal* 131, no. 3 (2006): 42–44.

Neal, James G. "The Research and Development Imperative in the Academic Library: Path to the Future." *portal: Libraries and the Academy* 6, no. 1 (2006): 1–3.

Postsecondary Education Opportunity. "State Tax Fund Appropriations for Higher Education FY1961 to FY2005." *Postsecondary Education Opportunity* 151 (2005): 1–20.

Sloan, Bernie. "Evolution Takes a Leap." *Netconnect*, April 2005 2–3.

University of California Libraries. "Rethinking How We Provide Bibliographic Services for the University of California." December 2005. http://libraries.universityofcalifornia.edu/sopag/BSTF/Final.pdf.

U.S. Department of Education. *A National Dialogue: The Secretary of Education's Commission on the Future of Higher Education, Issue Paper, "Frequently Asked Questions About College Costs,"* by Robert C. Dickeson. Washington, DC: U.S. Department of Education. 2006. http://www.ed.gov/about/bdscomm/list/hiedfuture/reports/dickeson2.pdf.

APPENDIX A

University of Arizona Libraries Overview of Digital Outreach Projects

The following is an overview of digital outreach projects that have been established or are planned at the University of Arizona (UA) Libraries.

Arizona Electronic Atlas (http://atlas.library.arizona.edu/).

The Arizona Electronic Atlas is a dynamic, Web-based, interactive state atlas that allows users to create, manipulate and download their own maps about natural resources, business and economics, the environment and the state's population, using all the latest data in the state.

A key purpose of the Atlas is to increase the geographic literacy of students. The Teaching Resources page of the Atlas includes learning modules and other resources to assist instructors in developing assignments using the Atlas. The learning modules are intended for undergraduate students, high school students, and the general public.

Use of the Arizona Electronic Atlas is free and it averages about 175 visits per day or 3600 per month. It has been integrated into several classes offered by the Departments of Geography and Regional Planning, the School of Planning, Ecology, and Natural Resources.

The Arizona-Sonora Desert Museum (ASDM) Online. The UA Libraries are collaborating with the museum to organize and provide access to the collections of the Arizona-Sonora Desert Museum, including slides of the terrestrial and aquatic species and habitats that are a part of the Sonora Desert region.

The digital library will be available in Spanish as well as English and will have tools for teachers and learners.

Center for Creative Photography Educator's Guides (http://www.creativephotography.org/education/guides.html).

Each year the Center for Creative Photography provides new teaching resources for elementary through college educators through its program of changing exhibitions. Educators across the curriculum are encouraged to explore exhibition images, issues, and related topics as opportunities for inquiry and interdisciplinary study both in the museum and within their classrooms. This series of guides offers educators everywhere images selected from the CCP collection and suggestions for integrating the exploration of photography and its fascinating range of artistic interpretations into diverse curricula.

Center for Creative Photography Exposure Project. This ambitious initiative is designed to create free public access to the collections, an interactive multimedia tour of the archives, and a guided educational experience about photographers' contributions to the history of the medium. The CCP's entire collection of 80,000 photographs and selections from the archives will be digitized. When the new website launches in 2009, a diverse global audience will be able to explore the CCP's collections with unprecedented ease and functionality.

GROW (http://www.grow.arizona.edu/). The Libraries have contributed to the Geotechnical, Rock & Water (GROW) Digital Library in collaboration with the Department of Civil Engineering at the University of Arizona. GROW is part of the National Science, Mathematics, and Technology Digital Library (NSDL). The GROW collection consists of 1,027 resources collected and developed by GROW team members in the areas of Geotechnical Engineering, Rock Engineering, and Water Resources.

GROW has had over 3 million visitors since March 2003, with an average of 3,300 page requests per day.

A K–12 area of the site offers selected resources for students and teachers at the elementary, middle, and high school levels.

Rangeland Monitoring in Western Uplands is an interactive Web-based learning module, complete with step-by-step activities and exercises. It was created by the University of Arizona's Range Extension Specialist (School of Natural Resources, College of Agriculture and Life Sciences), in collaboration with Office of Arid Lands Studies' Web designers and University of Arizona librarians. The project was funded by the National Learning Center for Private Forest and Range Landowners at the University of Tennessee, which is supported by the USDA, Cooperative State Research, Extension, and Education Service.

The Arid Lands Information Center is currently working on a second learning module for forestandrange.org—this one on invasive weeds—due to be completed in September.

Tree of Life (http://www.tolweb.org/). The Tree of Life (ToL) Project is a collaborative effort of biologists from around the world. On more than 4,000 World Wide Web pages, the project provides information about the diversity of organisms on Earth, their evolutionary history (phylogeny), and characteristics. The Libraries have been involved in the database design and ongoing technical support for the Tree of Life Project. Libraries staff are currently working with ToL on metadata and learning materials development.

The Tree of Life invites learners of all ages to explore Life on Earth and help the ToL create an open access digital library about biodiversity. Teachers, learners and science enthusiasts can contribute media to the ToL and build ToL treehouses.

Treehouses are Web pages about organisms and can be investigations, fun and games, stories, art and culture pieces, teacher resources, and biographies. Treehouses are linked to scientist-created core content pages. Treehouse building is an inquiry-based activity: teachers and learners choose their own topic, document their work and share it with a community of science practitioners by publishing it on the ToL.

Special Collections Online Exhibits (http://www.library.arizona.edu/speccoll/).

UA Libraries Special Collections offer twelve online exhibits, many of which provide special resources for students and teachers in K–12 schools. For example:

Little Cowpuncher, an exhibit of the rural Arizona school newspaper, was chosen as a Governor's Statehood Week Project for Fourth Graders. The newspaper consists of original and unedited stories and drawings that vividly describe the lives of schoolchildren throughout the school year at Redington, Baboquivari, Sasco, San Fernando, and Sopori schools.

The Bisbee Deportation of 1917 exhibit includes a section developed to assist teachers from grades 6–12 to teach about the Bisbee Deportation of 1917 and the related history of labor relations in the copper mining industry in the early twentieth century.

Support for English Composition Courses. The library has created an instructional support site for the English Composition instructors (http://aquarius.library.arizona.edu/services/faculty/engl102/index.html). The site offers instructional activities and ideas that integrate into the course curriculum by week. It also gives examples of how to add library information and research activities into the three major course assignments.

A companion site for English Composition students was created (http://www.library.arizona.edu/help/tutorials/courses/engl/102/). This site includes tutorials and guides that instructors can assign to their students as well as a link to the Chapter on Research from one of the course textbooks, *The Student's Guide to First Year Composition.*

Additional Digital Projects at the UA Libraries

Agriculture Network Information Center—Western Rangelands (http://rangelandswest.org). The UA Libraries have contributed to this site as part of a partnership to deliver quality information, resources, and tools to improve management and ensure sustainability of western rangelands. The goal of the project is to provide a comprehensive Web resource about science, management, and other issues related to Western rangelands. The increased availability of rangelands information by means of this regional system directly enhances the ability of people living, working, and interested in Arizona and western states to respond to environmental concerns and issues related to rangelands that are key to life and livelihoods in the western United States.

Arizona Archives Online (http://aao.lib.asu.edu). We collaborate with Arizona State University and Northern Arizona University to provide online, searchable access to finding aids for archival collections through the Arizona Archives Online (AAO) database.

Currently 194 of Special Collections' finding aids are in AAO, and more will be added as collections are processed.

Use for 2004–2005 was 8,812 unique visitors and 21,933 visits. A total of 582,915 pages were viewed.

Arizona-Sonora Documents Online (http://content.library.arizona.edu/collections/asdo). Arizona-Sonora Documents Online (ASDO) provides Web access to digital images of archival collections relating to Sonora, Mexico that are located at three Arizona repositories: the University of Arizona Library Special Collections; the Arizona Historical Society–Tucson; and the Arizona State Library, Archives, and Public Records. The collections date from the 19th and early 20th centuries and cover a broad range of topics, including ranching, mining, land grants, anti-Chinese movements, crime on the border, and governmental issues. ASDO uses ContentDM software.

This project was launched with a $200,000 grant from the Institute of Museum and Library Services in 2000.

The site has had approximately 5,000 unique visitors since 2002.

Books of the Southwest (http://www.library.arizona.edu/exhibits/swetc/). In 1996, the Libraries began presenting full-length books and pamphlets documenting Arizona and southwest history and culture on the Web. Many of these items are fragile and, prior to their online appearance, only available through an in-person visit to the Special Collections department. There are now forty-two items in this collection.

The texts of these titles were converted directly to HTML text pages and the original images included. Each text is intended to be easily accessible in a design that approximates the original book.

Electronic Theses and Dissertations (ETD). ETD is currently in creation to provide open access to UA electronic theses and dissertations, funded partially by submitted students' dissertation fees. To accomplish this we are joining with the Networked Digital Library of Theses and Dissertations (NDLTD), a distributed digital repository. NDLTD will provide searching capability for metadata from university libraries across the country. Cost is estimated at $30/dissertation times, and with approximately four hundred Ph.D.-earning students per year this would be $12,000 annually.

We will host our own files for this project; ETD will be offered in addition to (not instead of) UMI/Proquest's database.

GPO Digital Repository (http://www.library.arizona.edu/about/libraries/govdocs). The Libraries instituted a three-year project involving library school students. The students harvest lost EPA documents from the Web and we supply URLs to the GPO to be catalogued. The UA Libraries' GPO Digital Repository serves the government information needs of the fifth U.S. Congressional district of Arizona.

Journal of Insect Science (http://www.insectscience.org/). The *Journal of Insect Science* is a free, online journal created and published from 2001–2005 by the UA Libraries and edited by Professor Henry Hagedorn, Entomology. *JIS* publishes papers in all aspects of the biology of insects and other arthropods from the molecular to the ecological. Its guiding principle is that academic institutions should be involved in publishing scholarly work with as few impediments as possible to free access to information. Individual authors retain copyright in their articles. Articles are presented in HTML and PDF formats.

JIS articles are listed in at least twelve indices, including Agricola, BioOne, BIOSIS, Cambridge Scientific Abstracts, Chemical Abstracts Service, Medline, and PubMed.

JIS has published nearly 150 articles in five volumes as of Fall 2005. During the calendar year 2004, the site saw about 73,000 requests for pdf files, or 200 per day.

Legacy Technical Reports. We are pursuing a project to provide open access to legacy technical reports (scientific, engineering, and medical research reports published by government agencies and research institutions) since 1885. We are working on a prototype digital repository and looking for potential partners in addition to GPO. The costs of this project will be minimal, as it will use our custom-built software and servers we already own.

Western Waters Digital Library (http://www.westernwater.org). The University of Arizona Libraries are participants in the initial projects with six other libraries. We are submitting water-related documents from the Udall Collection and materials related to Native American Water Rights. We have contributed $20,000 to the project.

Responding to the Preservation Challenge: Portico, an Electronic Archiving Service

Eileen G. Fenton

ABSTRACT. The preservation of physical materials has traditionally connected users to content. Today libraries face new challenges as they address mission-critical digital preservation. To achieve long-term preservation of e-resources, libraries need to: act now to be a part of at least one e-journal preservation program; recognize that digital preservation requires multiple methodologies; and recognize that the scale of the challenge requires multiple actors. Portico, which provides robust digital preservation of electronic scholarly resources, is one element of the emerging digital preservation infrastructure. Portico is a community-based, third party archive that brings together scholarly publishers and libraries from around the world.

KEYWORDS. Portico, digital preservation, e-journals

INTRODUCTION

In the late 1980s I was fortunate enough to work at the Yale University Library in an office tucked away in a corner of Sterling Memorial Library. When I needed a break I would walk from the office, down a well-worn stone corridor, and make my way to Sterling's grand and (at the time) somewhat dusty stacks. With no particular destination in mind I would enter the stacks and browse the rich collection of materials on Sterling's aged shelving. I found something fascinating in the diversity in age, subject, binding, and style of the materials quietly resting in the stacks. My random walks in the stacks provided me with a vivid reminder of the grand purpose of an academic library collection, to gather materials together and preserve them over time so that at the right moment—tomorrow, next month, or decades hence—they might help a user make a new insight, theory or discovery, and further scholarship. The idea of the library struck me then, and does still today, as a wonderfully audacious proposition, astonishing for the rich possibilities that it holds.

During the 1980s, Yale's wonderful collection, like many other libraries, was under assault from a variety of forces: aging buildings, uncertain budgets, shrinking staff, as well as routine stress and strain from users. But libraries have always found ways to continue to connect users to their collections despite these assaults. For print materials one necessary step in ensuring the ongoing connection of users to materials has been the local effort to ensure the long-term preservation of the physical items—local preservation of print materials has traditionally been an important step to ensure access.

The Changing Landscape of Preservation

My fascination with library collections that await connection to users is what draws me to the digital preservation challenge that faces the higher education community today. In today's landscape, so radically altered by the prevalence of electronic information resources, libraries face new challenges and opportunities as they address the mission-critical preservation task. To be sure, some of the challenges are quite familiar: pressured budgets, uncertain funding from state legislatures or central administrations, and staff pulled in many directions. There are, however, at least three new elements in the current landscape that impact libraries' ability to successfully carry out the preservation of digital resources that is a necessary precursor to connecting users to digital content over the long term.

The first element in this changing landscape of preservation is the increasing portion of a library collection that is now comprised of licensed, not owned, electronic materials. This shift is illustrated most dramatically through the adoption of electronic journals. By 2004, members of the Association of Research Libraries (ARL) were devoting on average 42 percent of their total serials expenditures on licensing electronic journals, a dramatic increase from the 5 percent typical in 1995.[1] In this changing landscape, it has been unclear what party can, will, or should be the guarantor of long-term preservation (and access) of this licensed e-journal content. But the long-term preservation of e-journals is a pressing concern and was given forceful expression in the statement "Urgent Action Needed to Preserve Scholarly Electronic Journals" issued in September 2005 by a working group of academic librarians, administrators, and others convened by The Andrew W. Mellon Foundation.[2] Now endorsed by the Association of Research Libraries (ARL), the Association of College and Research Libraries (ACRL), and others, the "Urgent Action" statement expresses clearly that "digital preservation represents one of the grand challenges facing higher education," and it calls libraries to actively support electronic-journal archiving initiatives.

The second element in the changing landscape of preservation is the surprising fragility and increasing complexity of electronic resources. Digital content is prone to loss through accident, byte corruption, format obsolescence, and changes in hardware and software environments. Over time, e-resources have become much more complex. As an example, e-journals are no longer simple electronic reproductions of their parallel print format; rather, they are increasingly innovative and creative incorporating video, audio, and datasets. The innovation will only accelerate as electronic publishing practices mature. The third element in the changing landscape of preservation is that the demands of preserving this fragile and innovative e-literature requires significant preservation infrastructure—including hardware, software, staff expertise, and organizational and financial resources necessary to reliably support the implementation of a preservation strategy over the long term. The infrastructure challenges of preserving electronic resources are quite different from those raised by the preservation of print resources, and the broad and growing range of electronic resources in need of preservation has created demands that readily exceed those that can be addressed by any single institution. This is a landscape quite different from the print preservation world we know so well, where generally individual libraries locally housed and preserved their collections. To be sure these local efforts have traditionally been supplemented by interlibrary loan and various sharing agreements, but in the world of print resources a library's community predominantly relied upon locally preserved and held collections.

Responding to the Changing Landscape of Preservation

Ensuring that users into the future remain connected to digital content requires that libraries find ways to address the preservation challenges that digital content and the shifting landscape presents. For e-journal preservation, solutions are beginning to emerge and there are practical steps that can now be taken—a point underscored in the recent Council on Library and Information Resources (CLIR) report, *E-Journal Archiving Metes and Bounds: A Survey of the Landscape*.[3] This report surveys twelve e-journal archiving initiatives and makes a number of recommendations to publishers and libraries—recommendations that have recently been endorsed by the ARL. At this time at least three practical actions can help meet the preservation challenge before us as we work to maintain the connection between users and content.

First, as the ARL's endorsement of the CLIR report notes, libraries should proactively act—now—to "support and participate in at least one trustworthy and effective e-journal archiving initiative" and urge publishers to do the same. Participation in cooperative preservation solutions is one means to widely share the costs of preserving this e-content that is of value to a very broad community.

Second, we should recognize that preservation of the diverse body of digital resources important to libraries (e-journals included) will require an array of technological and organizational approaches. One single approach will not address the full complement of challenges and preservation needs of disparate digital resources (datasets, electronic records, e-journals, e-books, student portfolios, faculty courseware, etc.) of interest to libraries. Over time the community will develop greater expertise in the skills required to preserve these varied genres, and we should expect that each may impose different preservation requirements. But we will not develop this expertise unless the community finds a way to act in support of multiple solutions. Perhaps not all institutions will have the resources—financial or human—to support multiple efforts, but collectively as a community it will be important to act in support of diverse approaches to the digital preservation challenge.

Finally, the scale of the preservation challenge—the quantity of content and its complexity—suggests that multiple preservation agents and solutions will be required. There is much to be preserved and the responsibility will need to be distributed among many parties, such as discipline-based efforts (for example, the ICPSR and arXive), national libraries caring for a wide range of digital cultural heritage assets (for example the National Library of the Netherlands), institutional repositories caring for assets local to an institution (for example, DSpace at MIT), and third-party efforts (for example, JSTOR, Portico and the Internet Archive). To ensure that this preservation network reliably meets accepted standards, it is important for the community to foster and support audit or certification procedures or organizations. In recent weeks, two important efforts on this front, have announced significant progress. The U.K.-based Digital Curation Centre (www.dcc.ac.uk) and Digital Preservation Europe (www.digitalpreservationeurope.eu) have released the toolkit, *Digital Repository Audit Method Based on Risk Assessment,* which is "intended to facilitate internal audit by providing repository administrators with a means to assess their capabilities, identify their weaknesses, and recognise their strengths."[4] In the United States, the Center for Research Libraries (CRL) and RLG Programs (a unit of the Online Computer Library Center [OCLC] Programs and Research division) announced the publication of *Trustworthy Repositories Audit & Certification: Criteria and Checklist, which* builds upon the work of the Research Libraries Group—National Archives and Records Administration Task Force on Digital Repository Certification. The work of the Task Force was "to develop criteria to identify digital repositories capable of reliably storing, migrating, and providing access to digital collections" and the CRL/RLG project has now taken this work forward by shaping a certification process.[5] Libraries will want to follow both of these efforts and consider how they can support and participate in this work, perhaps by selecting archival efforts that meet the criteria identified in these programs.

One Model: An Overview of Portico

Practical responses to these changes in the preservation landscape can take shape in a variety of ways, and as we have crafted Portico's approach to preservation of electronic journals we have tried to be mindful of these shifts in the landscape. In pursuit of our mission to preserve scholarly literature published in electronic form and to ensure that these materials remain accessible to future generations of scholars, researchers, and students, we have developed, with input from publishers and libraries, one practical model for addressing the community's need for long-term preservation of electronic journal resources.

Portico provides a permanent archive of electronic scholarly journal literature. The Portico archive, which is a centralized and replicated repository, is open to a publisher's complete list of scholarly (peer-reviewed) journals, including those titles that may be published in electronic format only, or print and electronic formats, or that may have been "reborn" or digitized from print. Portico is focused on preserving the intellectual content of the electronic scholarly journal. Portico's archival approach for electronic journals is focused on the publishers' e-journal source files—the electronic files containing graphics, text, or other material that comprise an electronic journal article, issue, or volume. Portico receives source files directly from the scholarly publishers who have agreed to contribute to the Portico archiving service, and Portico has chosen migration as its primary long-term archival approach, as part of a managed preservation strategy.[6] Consistent with that approach, when files are received in proprietary formats or formats that are already deemed obsolete or unstable, they are pre-emptively normalized to an archival format to facilitate preservation and future migration.

Accessing the Archive

Portico recognizes that while access to e-journal literature today may not be a concern, librarians and their constituents must be confident in their ability to provide access to today's e-journal literature in the future. To address this need, all libraries supporting the Portico archive will have campus-wide access to archived content when specific trigger events occur, *and* when titles are no longer available from the publisher or other source. Trigger events include:

- A publisher ceases operations; or
- A publisher ceases to publish and offer a title; or
- A publisher no longer offers back issues; or
- Upon catastrophic and sustained failure of a publisher's delivery platform.

In addition to these trigger events, both publishers and libraries have recognized that after a library has terminated a license to an electronic resource, it may be necessary for that library to continue to have ongoing access to the content it had previously paid for and licensed. This is commonly known as perpetual or post-cancellation access. Portico is prepared to provide post-cancellation access for those publishers that choose to designate Portico a mechanism that they will use to meet this need, and at present twenty-seven of thirty-one publisher participants have made this designation.

As it is important that all parties be confident in the long-term accessibility of this preserved content, select librarians at participating libraries are granted password-controlled access to the content in the archive for verification purposes. This verification access, which is granted to all content preserved in the archive, is not intended to compete with publishers' current products and it may not be used as a replacement for commercial document delivery services. Finally, all publishers participating in the archive have full access to their own content.

The Role of Publishers and Libraries

Archiving cannot be accomplished without the cooperation and participation of the content owners—publishers—but because archiving is not necessarily core to a publisher's mission, it is important to keep barriers to participation in archival arrangements as low as possible. One way in which Portico achieves this is by agreeing to receive source files in whatever format is most convenient to the publisher and placing the responsibility for content normalization upon Portico.

To participate in Portico, a publisher:

- Signs a non-exclusive archiving license that gives Portico the right to ingest, normalize, archive, and migrate the publisher's content;
- Indicates whether Portico will serve as a post-cancellation access mechanism;
- Supplies electronic journal source files in a timely way; and
- Makes an annual financial contribution.

While preservation may not be mission critical for publishers, it is at the heart of the work of many libraries. As the "Urgent Action" statement makes clear, preservation of *electronic* resources is especially important for libraries. Although electronic resources have raised new preservation challenges, they also have generated new opportunities and today libraries can effect the preservation of electronic journals by supporting collaborative efforts. By supporting collaborative efforts like Portico, libraries and publishers can together contribute toward a shared infrastructure that supports a mutually beneficial and valued goal—the long-term, robust preservation of scholarly literature published in electronic form.

To participate in the Portico archive, a library:

- Signs an archiving license agreement;
- Makes an annual support payment; and
- Upon request, provides IP addresses or other relevant information necessary for the user authentication required to enable access.

Sustaining the Archive

Financial support is critical to a long-term preservation effort of any kind, and Portico intends to cover its ongoing operating costs from diversified funding sources. The chief beneficiaries of the archive—publishers and libraries—will provide the primary sources of funding to support ongoing operations. Portico will also seek additional support from charitable foundations and government agencies, primarily to fund capital investments. The annual publisher contribution to the archive is based on publishers' total journals revenues (subscription, advertising, licensing) and range from $250 to $75,000 per year. The annual library payments are tiered and they vary according to a library's (self-reported) total Library Materials Expenditure (LME) in order to reflect Portico's value in preserving a growing portion of a library collection. Library fees range from $1,500 to $24,000 per annum. To encourage broad participation in Portico from the outset, Portico designates early participants (institutions who begin Portico support in 2006 and 2007) as "Portico Archive Founders," and recognizes their early support of this important initiative by providing significant savings on Founders' annual support fees for the first five years (10 percent for libraries beginning participation in 2007). In addition, modest savings are offered to university systems and to members of consortia that work with Portico to share information with their member institutions.

Community Reactions

Though it is a young enterprise, Portico has made significant progress toward securing critical support from scholarly publishers and a significant, and growing, number of academic libraries. Since introducing Portico to publishers in late 2005 and through mid-February 2007, more than 5,800 journals have been promised to the archive from thirty-two publishers from across the spectrum. Participating publishers include large commercial publishers (e.g., Elsevier), university presses (e.g., University of California), scholarly societies (e.g., American Mathematical Society), and small scholarly publishers (e.g., Berkeley Electronic Press).[7] At the close of 2006, more than 343,000 articles from 587 titles had been preserved. The initial group of Portico library participants, or "Archive Founders," is also remarkable. At the close of 2006, 351 libraries were eligible for this designation, covering a spectrum of institutions from small liberal arts colleges to large university systems. Interestingly, almost 25 percent of the participation from this initial group came from eight countries outside the United States.[8]

While Portico offers one model to address the community's long-term preservation needs, the *E-Journal Metes and Bounds* report makes clear there are other models as well. Fostering multiple approaches—both technological and organizational—is one key way to avoid the potentially unacceptable risks that may come with placing all electronic resources in the care of a single digital preservation strategy.

CONCLUSION

Portico's day-to-day work of preservation—selecting an archival methodology, building a technical and organizational infrastructure, ingesting and managing content, developing and implementing archival policies—is all only a means to an end: ensuring that content is preserved for the very long term. This long-term preservation is only one part of the effort required to ensure that users remain connected to content. We are pleased to have the opportunity to work with publishers and libraries to ensure that content is well preserved, and we look forward to continuing to play a supporting role in the ongoing effort to ensure that users can remain connected over the long term to the dynamic, complex world of digital information resources.

NOTES

1. Kyrillidou, Martha, and Mark Young. 2005. *ARL Library Trends*. Washington, D.C.: Association of Research Libraries. http://www.arl.org/stats/arlstat/04pub/04intro.html (Accessed November 8, 2006).

2. Waters, Donald, ed. 2005. "Urgent Action Needed to Preserve Scholarly Journals." Available at http://www.diglib.org/pubs/waters051015.htm. (Accessed November 10, 2006).

3. The full report is available at http://www.clir.org/PUBS/abstract/pub138abst.html (Accessed February 28, 2007).

4. The toolkit is available at http://www.repositoryaudit.eu/ (Accessed March 6, 2007).

5. The revised checklist is available at http://bibpurl.oclc.org/web/16712 (Accessed March 9, 2007).

6. Migration involves transitioning content from one file format to another as technology evolves and file formats become obsolete. Two other common preservation strategies include emulation, which involves strategies to make future technology mimic technology of earlier generations, and byte preservation, which involves simple storage of an unmodified stream of digital data without special provision for future display or functionality.

7. A full list of committed titles is available at http://www.portico.org/about/committed_titles_alpha.html and publishers at http://www.portico.org/about/part_publishers.html.

8. Library participants come from Australia, Canada, Cyprus, Greece, India, Sweden, the United States, and the United Kingdom.

Assessing the Value and Impact of Digital Content

Brinley Franklin
Terry Plum

ABSTRACT. During the last decade, library users have responded favorably to the rapid growth in available digital content. In recent years, a number of assessment initiatives related to digital content have surfaced. Among these are projects to standardize the measurement of digital content use, user satisfaction with digital content, cost/benefit analyses, and determination of the demographics and purpose of use of digital content. This paper surveys early attempts by libraries to assess the value and impact of digital content on users. It also explores the potential that digital content offers libraries for understanding library usage, which previously was not available in the traditional print environment.

KEYWORDS. Digital content, networked services, electronic information, measurement, value, impact, assessment, evaluation, cost/benefit, user studies

Digital content affords librarians the ability to understand networked services usage in a way that was not previously possible in the traditional print library environment. As library users have responded favorably to the rapid growth of available digital content during the last decade, a number of assessment initiatives emerged that improve our knowledge of how library resources are actually being used.

In the print environment, online public access catalogs provided only limited management information about circulating materials. In-house library collections usage statistics were unreliable. Journal use surveys, based on self-reported checklists or re-shelving counts, were unconvincing. In truth, librarians never completely understood how print collections were used. The digital content environment affords libraries unprecedented opportunities to measure, assess, and analyze networked services use.

Projects are now under way to standardize measures of digital content use and to assess its value, including: user satisfaction with networked resources, cost/benefit ratios, return on investments, and determinations of how specific user populations apply digital content to their work, based on demographic and purpose of use analyses. Electronic services use data is being collected not only for collections management decisions, but to justify increased funding for digital content, to craft library services in new ways, to inform management decisions, and to assert the impact of networked electronic resources and services on teaching, learning, and research.

TRADITIONAL PRINT COLLECTION USE IN THOSE "MILES OF AISLES"

About a decade into the digital information environment, we already know considerably more about digital content use than we ever did about print journal and book use. In previous decades, librarians conscientiously counted outputs including circulating library materials, reference and information questions, and interlibrary loans, even though the data collected, in retrospect, was unreliable and, most likely, inconsistent, due to varying loan periods, local practices regarding how to count informational and directional versus reference questions, and variances in how libraries classified interlibrary loans as opposed to circulation transactions. Journal review projects were transparently aimed at canceling titles and were subject to manipulation.

Librarians collected usage data, when they were: (a) interested in measuring their libraries' performance, (b) asked to compile statistics for professional associations or governmental agencies, or (c) confronted with budget cuts. They typically relied on gross circulation counts and routinely employed unscientific and unreliable sampling plans and primitive in-house data collection methods such as asking users not to re-shelve library materials so the library could count them. These "usage studies" purported to measure library collections use when in fact there was never any tangible proof or consistent interpretation of what a book being removed from the shelf, or even a circulating item, really represented.

It is telling that the authors of one of the most commonly cited articles on print collection use in an academic library, published in 1977 and aptly titled, "Use of a University Library Collection" observed that:

> The gross data available up to this point have been too global in character and too imprecise in nature to serve as an adequate basis for the reformulation of acquisitions policies. It is not particularly helpful for a bibliographer to know that ten percent of the titles selected will satisfy 90 percent of client demand for materials in a given discipline, unless we can determine which ten percent. It is useless to tell the acquisitions librarian that half the monographs ordered will never be used, unless we can specify which 50 percent to avoid buying.[1]

As recently as 2003, a Mellon Foundation-funded study by the Tri-College Library Consortium (Bryn Mawr, Haverford, and Swarthmore Colleges) done in conjunction with the Council on Library and Information Resources found that approximately 75 percent of the items in the three libraries' collections had circulated one or fewer times in the past ten years. Also, about 40 percent of the items in the collections overlapped (i.e., they were held on more than one campus). About half of these overlapping items had not circulated in the past eleven years.[2]

In retrospect, collection development in the print environment was more of an art than a science. Libraries knew how much they were spending, but were unable to ascertain how their collections were being used or how to use the data they could collect to better inform purchasing decisions.

THE BRAVE NEW WORLD OF DIGITAL CONTENT, NEW MEASURES, AND E-METRICS

In January 1999, Carla Stoffle, the Dean of Libraries at the University of Arizona and Chair of the Association of Research Libraries' (ARL) Statistics and Measurement Committee, invited members from ARL's Statistics and Measurement Committee and the ARL Management Committee to Tucson to discuss the concept of "New Measures." This retreat was in response to: (1) increased demand for libraries to demonstrate outcomes and impacts (instead of inputs and outputs) important to their institution and (2) increasing budgetary and political pressure to maximize efficient use of resources and to identify best practices.[3]

Ultimately, the "New Measures" initiatives that Carla Stoffle set in motion resulted in several assessment tools sponsored by ARL libraries that began to assess the new world of digital content. These included: Project SAILS (Standardized Assessment of Information Literacy Skills) in partnership with Kent State University, and electronic resources measures (E-Metrics), developed by a group of twenty-four sponsoring ARL libraries under a contract with Florida State University's (FSU) Information Use Management and Policy Institute and under the leadership of project co-chairs Sherrie Schmidt, Dean of Libraries at Arizona State University and Rush Miller, University Librarian at the University of Pittsburgh. As two of the FSU consultants, Chuck McClure and Jeff Wonsik Shim, reported: "The proliferation of networked electronic information resources and services prompted interest and research in developing statistics and measures to describe this emerging information provision environment."[4]

The task was not an easy one. Among the challenges documented by Sherrie Schmidt and Rush Miller were:

lack of clear and consistent definition of data elements;
vendors do not "count" things in the same manner as one another;
membership in a consortium can skew the statistics of the individual libraries in that consortium;
libraries structure themselves differently in regard to electronic resources, making data gathering difficult;
libraries do not control access to and use of important data about vendor-supplied resources; and
the nature of electronic resources is changing rapidly and therefore data elements are shifting.[5]

ARL's E-Metrics project resulted in nineteen data elements representing four categories: (1) Number of Networked Electronic Resources, (2) Expenditures for Networked Electronic Resources, (3) Use of Networked Electronic Resources and Services, and (4) Library Digitization Activities. As described by ARL's Director of Information Services, Julia Blixrud, in 2002:

The ARL E-Metrics project has been only a beginning, but it is a significant undertaking to identify the measures needed to provide information on the electronic resources libraries provide to their communities. The project demonstrated that the collection of data to provide that information is a complex set of activities, and requires the cooperation of many units within a library and of the vendors who produce the products and services that the libraries make available.... ARL will continue to search for the best measures to determine how the provision of electronic resources contributes to the success of library users.[6]

The E-Metrics developed by ARL in 2002 by twenty-four of its members became ARL's *Supplementary Statistics* in 2003–2004. The ARL *Supplementary Statistics* serve as an experimental compilation to collect information on new measures. These *Supplementary Statistics* have yielded valuable public services and government documents' measures in the past, and currently are being used to normalize statistical measures related to electronic resources. During the next several years, some of the nineteen E-Metrics data elements developed by ARL in conjunction with FSU will most likely be deemed "mature" enough to move into the main ARL Statistics questionnaire. Others, in all likelihood, will not be determined significant enough in value or sufficiently normalized as accurate counts and will be withdrawn from consideration.[7]

VENDOR SUPPLIED DATA AND TRANSACTION BASED USAGE

Currently, the most common approach to measuring digital content usage is based on vendor-supplied data or, less often, transaction-based usage. A number of standards-setting groups have developed guidelines for setting consistent measures of digital content usage across different publishers and products, including: Project COUNTER, or Counting Online Usage of NeTworked Electronic Resources (http://www.projectcounter.org); the International Coalition of Library Consortia, or ICOLC (http://www.library.yale.edu/consortia); the International Organization for Standardisation, or ISO, 11620 *Library Performance Indicators* (http://www.iso.org); and the National Information Standards Organization, or NISO, Z39.7 *Library Statistics* (http://ww.niso.org).

Despite Stemper and Jaguszewski's assertion in 2003 that: "vendor-supplied e-resource statistics are often unavailable, unreliable, or not comparable across vendors,"[8] these standardization efforts have encouraged many publishers to become COUNTER-compliant. In a complementary development, NISO is sponsoring and formalizing the work of a committee that is developing a standard, SUSHI, or the Standardized Usage Statistics Harvesting Initiative (http://www.niso.org/committees/SUSHI/) for moving Project COUNTER usage statistics into a digital repository. Adam Chandler (Cornell University) and Oliver Pesch (Ebsco Information Services) are co-chairing the committee, which, according to its Web site, consists of "a cross-industry group of solution-seekers."[9]

These issues of concern to librarians and publishers related to the standardized development and interpretation of statistics that surfaced at approximately the same time electronic journals began to gain popularity.[10] Libraries and particularly consortia that host electronic resources on their own servers face the same issues in collecting usage statistics as publishers and, increasingly, libraries are offering locally mounted digital collections and services, the usage of which they would like to effectively measure.

A useful survey of data collection related to networked resources use at the local library level can be found in White and Kamal's 2006 monograph on using e-metrics to manage and evaluate electronic resources collections. The University of Pennsylvania Library, for example, under the leadership of Joe Zucca, has created the Penn Library Data Farm, which combines locally harvested e-journal and database use with other data elements to form a library management information system.[11]

Stemper and Jaguszewski demonstrated in 2003 that "local use data allows us to compare usage across publishers and disciplines." They concluded that "it may be useful to occasionally compare local statistics with vendor statistics to understand usage in more depth" and "both local and vendor usage data have their own strengths and weaknesses.... Both have their place in the digital library's suite of quantitative evaluation measures."[12]

The increased standardization of vendor-supplied data and the development of sophisticated collection mechanisms for measuring usage by the local library or consortium will no doubt continue on mutually beneficial tracks into the foreseeable future. The development of library portal technologies such as frameworks incorporating the Joint Information Systems Committee Information Architecture Environment, or JISC IE, (http://www.ukoln.ac.uk/distributed-systems/jisc-ie/

arch/) or the IMS Digital Repositories Framework (http://www.imsproject.org/digitalrepositories) and the development of library gateways[13] will only encourage standardization in collecting digital content usage data from both local and remote servers.

COST-BENEFIT ANALYSES/UNIT COSTS AND IMPROVED COLLECTIONS MANAGEMENT PRACTICES

Galvin and Kent referred to the book budget in the academic world as "the most sacred of sacred cows" and pointed out:

> The hard facts are that research libraries invest very substantial funds to purchase books and journals that are rarely, or never, called for as well as equally large sums to construct and maintain buildings designed to make accessible quickly titles that are no longer either useful to or sought by their clientele.[14]

Fortunately, digital content now allows us to analyze its use and determine cost-benefit analyses and unit costs and to parlay that information into more data-driven library collections management practices.

Cost-Benefit Analyses/Unit Cost Data

In the past, when librarians pondered the benefit of purchasing library materials against their cost, they relied on book circulation data, in-house journal use studies, or anecdotal user testimonies. Interlibrary loan requests, at least, were sometimes used to identify materials that would be more cost effective to own. Now, most libraries employ cost-benefit techniques to determine whether digital content is used often enough to justify its cost. Many libraries perform this cost-benefit analysis on the basis of unit costs.[15]

Three ground-breaking cost-benefit analysis studies occurred between 2002 and 2004. The first, conducted at Drexel University and reported on by Carol Montgomery and Donald King, determined that, while not directly comparable, the total costs (subscription and operational) of electronic journals calculated on a cost-per-use basis were $1.85 per use, compared to $17.50 per use for print journals. These calculations were based on article views and downloads for electronic journals and four years of re-shelving counts for print journals. Electronic journal use was also much higher than the print journal use measured.[16]

A second study, performed by Oliver Obst at the Medical Branch Library of the University Library in Muenster, Germany in 2003, only considered subscription costs. Obst's study also determined considerably lower unit costs for electronic journal use (€3.47) than print journal use (€18.68). Consistent with Montgomery and King's findings, users accessed the electronic versions of journals much more frequently than the print versions. The Muenster study also found significant differences in unit costs by publisher.[17]

A third study, published by the Council on Library and Information Resources in 2004, considered the non-subscription costs of current print journals, print journal back files, and electronic journals. This study was interesting in that it attempted to project cost over the estimated total life span for periodicals. Again, the authors concluded that, "other things being equal, an electronic collection should achieve lower non-subscription costs than a print collection."[18]

Cost and use data is relatively easy to compile for digital resources. With most vendor-supplied and transaction-based usage counts, digital content usage data are based upon total usage for a given year, not a sample. Any estimates for comparable print journal usage data are usually derived from a sample. The data collected to-date indicates that the cost per use of an article in an electronic journal is fairly inexpensive. The more often that digital content is used, the lower the unit cost, and the resulting increase in perceived value to the user population reflected by increased use does not incur additional cost. Therefore, offering digital content encourages the development of library services such as marketing, instruction, and liaison outreach. Moving to digital content also nurtures the development of new technology systems to leverage already committed expenses, such as OpenURL, Web usability studies, and electronic resource management systems.

Collections Management Practices

With respect to evaluating print collection usage, Galvin and Kent asserted that: "the available data lack sufficient predictive power to enable the librarian to modify selection practices with assurance that the results will be more responsive to future client needs."[19]

Now, consortia like the Ohio Library and Information Network, or OhioLINK (http://www.ohiolink.edu/), and the Ontario Council of

University Libraries, or OCUL (http://www.ocul.on.ca/), mount commercially licensed digital content locally and calculate cost-per-use data by title, by publisher, and by member library to determine which electronic resources merit continuation of their licensing and operational costs. Individual libraries measure total use of individual electronic resources and packages and calculate unit costs, usually based on vendor-supplied usage data, to decide which titles and packages have a low enough unit cost to warrant continued investment.

The University of Connecticut Networked Services Team annually calculates unit costs for electronic journals and databases and uses that information to inform collection development decisions. Unit cost analysis can help to determine whether publishers' cost increases are justified with increases in usage growing faster than the costs are inflating. While unit cost data should not be the sole determinant in buying decisions, it does provide data that can be used to explain to faculty and students why a title or package may not be a good investment at their university. Unit cost data also standardizes different publishers, vendors, and products so that titles and packages can be evaluated effectively.

As librarians at the University of Montana reported in 2004:

> For the first time, the Collection Development Team was able to review the networked resources collection from an overview of quantitative data and relate it to the collection development policy.... At the same time, national-level initiatives to work with vendors to standardize vendor-supplied data provide the future opportunity to further expand the analysis to include how users actually use these resources once they are accessed.[20]

WEB-BASED USAGE SURVEYS

In addition to vendor-supplied data and locally generated transaction usage, Web-based usage surveys are increasingly relevant in the refinement of collection development and service decisions. Web-based surveys can be used to:

document usage by specific user groups;
determine which of the electronic services a library offers are critical to instruction/education, funded research, patient care, public service, and other institutional missions; and
assess the perceived impact of digital resources and services.

Vendor-supplied data and transaction counts are typically a census of all electronic resource usage during a specific time period. Most Web-based surveys are samples and require a scientific sampling plan to ensure validity and reliability. Achieving participation by a representative sample of users is important and the introduction of bias into the survey instrument and the sample must be minimized.

One way to reduce the effect of non-respondents is to survey the user when the digital resource is selected for viewing. For Web-based surveys of electronic services usage that attempt to intercept the user at the point of use, inclusiveness is an important factor, and the methodology for determining at what point in the session and by what meansthe survey instrument is presented to the user are critical. If a redirect to the survey is placed after one of the library's Web pages and just before the user connects to the desired electronic resource or service, for example, the user who does not access the electronic resource or service through the library's Web page (e.g., through a bookmark or a departmental Web page) will not be included in the sample. In that case, the survey will be biased in that it is really only measuring electronic services users who access electronic services through the library's Web pages.

StatsQUAL™

Since ARL's development of E-Metrics in 2002, its focus has expanded to include three Web-based survey protocols. Questions related to digital content are part of the most commonly used instrument to measure library user satisfaction, LibQUAL +®, or LibQUAL. LibQUAL +® is a gap-analysis tool, administered to identify perceptions of service quality and gaps between desired, perceived, and minimum expectations of library service. It is delivered through a remotely hosted Web site and is promoted locally through email, campus announcements, posters, and other marketing efforts to encourage participation.

A second protocol, DigiQUAL™, or DigiQUAL, measures user satisfaction with various digital libraries. It is aimed at users who are using specific, closed digital library environments, and the survey is delivered at the point of use of the digital library, rather than within the specific resources contained in that particular digital library.

A third Web-based user survey methodology is MINES for Libraries™ (MINES). MINES was adopted by the Association of Research Libraries (ARL) as part of the "New Measures" toolkit in May 2003. MINES is different from electronic resource usage measures that quantify and set digital content usage standards (e.g., ProjectCOUNTER, E-Metrics, the ICOLC Guidelines, and ISO and NISO standards) or measure how well a library makes electronic resources (LibQUAL +®) or digital library services accessible (DigiQUAL +™). MINES, as currently implemented, collects demographic data about electronic resources' users, users' locations at the time of use, and their purpose of use. It is delivered at the point of use of an e-journal, database, article, digital collection, or digital library service. Collectively, LibQUAL +® DigiQUAL™ and MINES for Libraries™ currently comprise ARL's StatsQUAL™ product offerings.

LibQUAL +®

LibQUAL has now been utilized by more than a thousand libraries worldwide and scores of articles related to LibQUAL have been published since it was adapted from the ServQUAL protocol at Texas A&M University and then pilot tested in 2000 by twelve ARL libraries (see www.libqual.org). Early in its development, LibQUAL was a relatively complicated survey with over fifty questions. It has been simplified over the years, and now has twenty-two core items that fall into three subscales: (1) Affect of Service, (2) Library as Place, and (3) Information Control.

Recently, three of the primary architects of the LibQUAL phenomenon, Bruce Thompson, Colleen Cook, and Martha Kyrillidou, authored an as yet unpublished LibQUAL +® study titled, "Library Users' Services Desires and Tolerances: A LibQUAL +® Study." This new study demonstrates that, of the twenty-two core items, the six most desired among the three academic library user groups (undergraduate students, graduate students, and faculty) in the United States are all part of the Information Control subscale. This finding is based on Web-based survey results from more than 225,000 LibQUAL +® participants in the United States in 2004, 2005, and 2006.

Thompson, Cook, and Kyrillidou report that the most desired core item was: *Making electronic resources accessible from my home or office.* This item ranked first among graduate students and second among undergraduate students and faculty. The second most desired core item was: *Print and/or electronic journal collections I require for my work.* It ranked first among faculty, second among graduate students, and fifth among undergraduates. The third most desired core item was: *A library Web site enabling me to locate information on my own.* This item ranked third among faculty and undergraduate students and fourth among graduate students.[21] Interestingly, all three of the most commonly identified desires are related to digital resources.

DigiQUAL™

DigiQUAL is a collaboration between ARL, Texas A&M, and the University of Texas that evaluates digital libraries from a user's perspective. It has been supported to-date with funding from the National Science Foundation's National Science Digital Library (NSDL) program. NSDL was created in 2000 to encourage innovations in teaching, research, and learning at all levels of science, technology, engineering, and mathematics.

DigiQUAL represents a modification of the LibQUAL +® protocol and employs five questions selected randomly from a possible 180 queries. In its initial implementation, DigiQUAL evaluated the services, functionality, and content of the Digital Library for Earth System Education (DLESE), the Computational Science Education Reference Desk (CSERD), Utopia, The Math Forum@Drexel, and the Multimedia Educational Resource for Learning and Online Testing.[22]

MINES for Libraries™

MINES, developed by the authors, is a Web-based transactional survey that collects data on users' demographics and their purpose of use. It is typically administered in real time over the course of a year using a random moments sampling plan. MINES has been administered at forty North American libraries in the last four years. More than 100,000 networked services users have been surveyed using a standard protocol at those forty universities since 2003.

Between 2003 and 2005, networked services users at thirty-three North American libraries were asked to identify their location, status, and purpose of use through the MINES protocol. At main libraries in the United States, for example, 64 percent of the 25,698 uses surveyed were by remote users (i.e., not inside the library). This percentage was even higher for the 31,883 academic health sciences library uses surveyed (79 percent) and roughly the same for the 20,300 uses surveyed at the Ontario Council of University Libraries (OCUL), where 80 percent of their uses were by remote users.[23]

It is important for library service development to note that although the usage of electronic resources is high from outside the library, there is also considerable undergraduate usage of electronic resources from within the main academic library. Many students are coming into the library not just to do email or to access non-academic Web sites; many also come to search for e-journal articles and other digital content offered by their libraries.

Analyzing location by status of user at main libraries in the United States, it was determined that the highest digital resources usage from inside the library was by undergraduates (43 percent), while on campus but not in the library, the largest user group was graduate students (40 percent of total use), followed by faculty and staff (31 percent), and then undergraduate students (25 percent).[24]

Overall, coursework was the most common purpose of use (42 percent) among the nineteen OCUL libraries, followed by sponsored research (26 percent) and non-sponsored research (16 percent).[25] The fact that slightly more than one quarter of all usage supported funded research, lent considerable support to OCUL's appeal to its provincial government to continue funding its Scholar's Portal initiative because funded researchers relied on its offerings to successfully compete for and carry out important research initiatives.

Overall use among the approximately 26,000 main campus library users surveyed in the United States was predominantly for instruction/coursework/unfunded research (62 percent), while funded research usage was approximately 11 percent of total use. Networked services use for instruction/coursework/unfunded research did not vary significantly by location (66 percent in the library, 63 percent on campus, but not in the library, and 58 percent off campus). The fact that 11 percent of networked services use was for sponsored research purposes is significant. Using MINES, cost and use data can be enriched by adding purpose of use data to assign a monetary value for the amount of an academic library's networked services expenses that support funded research.

At main libraries in the United States, usage related to funded research varied more significantly by location, ranging from 21 percent on campus, but not in the library, to about 5 percent in the library and 6 percent off campus. At these main libraries, 72 percent of electronic services use supporting funded research occurred outside the library, but 83 percent of this funded research-related remote use took place on campus. At U.S. medical libraries 83 percent of electronic services use supporting funded research occurred outside the library, but 92 percent of the funded research-related remote use took place on (rather than off) campus.[26]

Recently, several implementations of MINES for Libraries™ have made significant advances in addressing the problem of capturing all electronic services users, not just those accessing digital content through the library's

Web pages. The first instance is an advanced application of EZproxy to present the MINES survey instrument to networked services users as they initiate a session. This development is noteworthy because it can be implemented by any library running EZproxy, and because it captures almost all of the networked services usage both locally and remotely during the sampled time periods.

EZproxy is authored by Chris Zagar, systems librarian at Estrella Mountain Community College, one of Arizona's Maricopa Community Colleges. As its Useful Utilities homepage[27] states, "Since 1999, EZproxy has provided the easiest way for libraries to extend web-based licensed databases to their remote users." EZproxy has subsequently been adopted by 1800 libraries in forty-six countries since its introduction in 1999. In June 2006, Chris Zagar was recognized with the Library and Information Technology Association/Brett Butler Entrepreneurship Award for developing an innovative product (EZproxy) designed to meet the needs of the library world.

As implemented at the University of Texas Medical Branch at Galveston (UTMB) in 2007, the auto-login banner shown to the patron by EZproxy at the first patron login redirects the user to the MINES survey at the appropriate (i.e., survey sample) times, using EZproxy 4.0g (beta). The patron completes the survey, and then is returned to the EZproxy login screen. Because there is a time-out period with EZproxy in which a login is not required, this method redirects the first URL access for proxied users, but not subsequent accesses by the same browser.

Don Brunder, Associate Director of Academic Computing, and his staff at UTMB took this methodology and added a line to the ezproxy.cfg to log all uses of the starting point URLs. These data are extracted from the log file through SQL. The end result is that all uses of networked electronic resources that pass through the EZProxy server, whether there is a login or not, are surveyed during the sampled time period. The time-out in the EZproxy cookie resets the survey when the patron is asked to log in again. This methodology is significant because of its potentially wide applicability: it can be implemented by any library running EZproxy, and it captures virtually all of the networked services usage during the sampled time periods. Further work on this approach is in progress.

Another solution to the problems of bookmarks and other non-surveyed usage in point-of-use surveys is to capture all usage of networked electronic resources at the campus Internet router. Jim Madden, Manager of Network Operations at the University of California–San Diego (UCSD), in collaboration with Steven Wieda, the UCSD Libraries' Web Managing Editor and a team of information technology specialists at the UCSD Libraries, developed an approach that picks up both on-campus users and off-campus users who come through the proxy server or virtual private network (VPN). This methodology captures all of the usage of networked electronic resources by authorized users during the randomly selected survey periods since it is administered at the router. It is an excellent example of cooperation between the campus network administrators and the library. The methodology will be explained by the UCSD team in a forthcoming publication.

CONCLUSION

Less than a decade into the assesment of digital content, measuring the value and impact of digital content already provides librarians with more useful and accurate data related to collections use than was possible in the print library environment. Measuring digital content use has evolved rapidly since 1999 to encompass initiatives to standardize counting of digital content use, compute unit cost data to reinforce the economic benefits of moving from print to electronic content, calculate local cost benefit analyses for specific titles and packages, gauge user satisfaction with digital content and digital libraries, and mine digital content usage to ascertain users' demographics, location, and purpose of use.

Recent refinement of Web-based survey techniques promises to provide librarians with even more representative and reliable samples of digital content use. Web-based surveys can be used to measure user satisfaction and digital library usage that is not vendor supplied, such as locally mounted digital collections and services and locally hosted open access journals. Surveying at the campus router level or at the proxy re-writer provides a comprehensive sampling plan that is able to survey all electronic services users, regardless of their point of entry.

These assessment efforts allow librarians to better understand digital content usage, make more informed collection development decisions, and to better justify collections management choices. Librarians are now able to more accurately determine who is using specific digital content. Knowing the locations where networked services are being used (e.g., the majority of faculty prefer to work on campus, but not in the library) enables librarians to plan user support services accordingly. Determining purpose of use permits academic librarians to identify which electronic resources contribute most to their institutions' primary missions of instruction/education/unfunded research; funded research; patient care; public service; and other institutional activities.

A decade into the electronic information environment, librarians are already far ahead of what they knew about print collections use. In the coming years, there will be further developments in Web survey techniques, further progress in the standardization, harvesting, and analysis of vendor-supplied and locally collected digital content usage data, and greater reliability and refinement of the digital content usage data that librarians will increasingly use for assessment, purchasing, and service decisions.

NOTES

1. Galvin, Thomas and Allen Kent, "Use of a University Library Collection." *Library Journal* 102.20 (1977): 2317–2320.

2. Luther, Judy, Linda Bills, Amy McColl, Norm Medeiros, Amy Morrison, Eric Pumroy, and Peggy Seiden. *Library Buildings and the Building of a Collaborative Research Collection at the Tri-College Library Consortium: Report to the Andrew W. Mellon Foundation*. Washington, D.C.: Council on Library and Information Resources, 2003.

3. Shepherd, Peter and Denise Davis, "Electronic Metrics, Performance Measures, and Statistics for Publishers and Libraries: Building Common Ground and Standards." *Portal: Libraries and the Academy* 2, no. 4 (2002):659–663.

4. Shim, Wonsik and Charles McClure, "Data Needs and Use of Electronic Resources at Academic Research Libraries." *Portal: Libraries and the Academy* 2, no. 2 (2002):217–236.

5. Miller, Rush and Sherrie Schmidt. "E-metrics: measures for electronic resources." In *Proceedings of the 4th Northumbria International Conference on Performance Measurement in Libraries and Information Services*, ed. Joan Stein, Martha Kyrillidou, and Denise Davis, 37–42 (Washington, D.C.: Association of Research Libraries 2002).

6. Blixrud, Jullia C. "Measures for Electronic Use: The ARL E-Metrics Project." *Paper presented at Statistics in Practice—Measuring and Managing*. IFLA pre-conference, Northumbria Lite, 2002.

7. http://www.arl.org/stats/annualsurveys/sup/index.shtml.

8. Stemper, James A. and Janice M. Jaguszewski, "Usage Statistics for Electronic Journals: An Analysis of Local and Vendor Counts." *Collection Management* 28, no. 4 (2003) 3–22.

9. http://www.niso.org/committees/SUSHI/SUSHI_comm.html.

10. Luther, Judy, *White Paper on Electronic Journal Usage Statistics*. Washington, D.C.: Council on Library and Information Resources (2000).

11. White, Andrew and Eric Djiva Kamal. *E-Metrics for Library and Information Professionals: How to Use Data for Managing and Evaluating Electronic Resources Collections*. New York: Neal Schuman (2006).

12. Stemper, James A. and Janice M. Jaguszewski. "Usage Statistics for Electronic Journals: An Analysis of Local and Vendor Counts." *Collection Management* 28, no. 4 (2003) 3–22.

13. Caswell, Jerry V. "A Conceptual Framework for Gateways." *Information Technology and Libraries* 23.2.(2004) 73–82.

14. Galvin and Kent, "Use of a University Library Collection." p. 2317.

15. Franklin, Brinley. "Managing the Electronic Collection with Cost per Use Data" *IFLA Journal* 31, no. 3 (2005): 241–248.

16. Montgomery, Carol Hanson and Donald W. King. "Comparing Library and User Related Costs of Print and Electronic Journal Collections: A First Step Towards a Comprehensive Analysis" *D-Lib Magazine* 8, no. 10 (2002).

17. Obst, Oliver. "Patterns and Cost of Printed and Online Journal Usage." *Health Information and Libraries Journal* 20 (2003): 22–32.

18. Schonfeld, Roger C., Donald W. King, Ann Okerson, and Eileen Gifford Fenton. *The Nonsubscription Side of Periodicals: Changes in Library Operations and Costs Between Print and Electronic Formats*. Washington, D.C.: Council on Library and Information Resources (2004).

19. Galvin and Kent, "Use of a University Library Collection." p. 2317.

20. Samson, Sue, Sebastian Derry, and Holly Eggleston. "Networked Resources, Assessment and Collection Development." *The Journal of Academic Librarianship* 30, no. 6 (2004): 476–481.

21. Thompson, Bruce, Colleen Cook, and Martha Kyrillidou. Library Users' Service Desires and Tolerances: A LibQUAL +® Study. 2007. Preprint.

22. Kyrillidou, Martha and Sarah Giersch. "Developing the DigiQUAL Protocol for Digital Library Evaluation." Paper presented at MERLOT International Conference, Nashville, TN, 2005.

23. Franklin, Brinley and Terry Plum. "Successful Web Survey Methodologies for Measuring the Impact of Networked Electronic Services (MINES for Libraries)." *IFLA Journal* 32, no. 1 (2006): 28–40.

24. Ibid.

25. Ibid.

26. Ibid.

27. www.usefulutilities.com.

All Hype or Real Change: Has the Digital Revolution Changed Scholarly Communication?

Barbara McFadden Allen

ABSTRACT. Digital and electronic publishing models offer the promise of revolutionary change in the way scholarly publications are created, accessed, and shared. However, real change in the scholarly communication system has lagged behind the availability of new publishing models for scholars. This paper describes some of the current trends in library acquisitions of electronic resources, as well as trends in scholar adoption of new publishing models. The author also suggests some strategies that libraries and universities might employ to accelerate a shift to a more open, effective means of sharing the results of research and scholarship.

KEYWORDS. Scholarly communication, digital libraries, electronic resources

I've had the privilege of engaging in conversations about the future of scholarly communications with university presidents, provosts, deans, librarians, faculty, and press directors. All of life's rich pageant has paraded before my eyes as these players have examined and discussed the opportunities and challenges presented by new modes of publishing and scholarly expression, and I've come to the conclusion that (as with so many things in life) those who walked before us really did understand the issues:

> For as long as any of us can remember, the system of scholarly communication has worked in the following way: Scholars toiled in the library or in their studies or by doing research in the field; they wrote what they had to say; the writings were judged by their peers; some writings fell by the wayside or went back for revision, but the best were published in books or journals; the books and journals were collected and arranged in libraries where other scholars could use them. It was a cyclical flow that continually renewed itself and enriched human knowledge and understanding. It was a good system and it worked well until recently.[1]

These words were penned not last week, or last year, or even five years ago, but comprise the summation of deliberations initiated by the American Council of Learned Societies the year I graduated from high school.

While I cannot pretend nor hope to understand all of the arguments and conversations underway regarding the system of scholarly communication, it seems to me that the economics of the system captures a large amount of attention, and I believe such a focus prevents us from thinking clearly and rationally. Worse, it pits natural friends and allies in the academy against one another. We focus too much attention fretting about the amount of money we are investing in the current system while criticizing the economic models of the emerging systems instead of thinking rationally—together—about the necessary investment in—or more importantly, the design of—the overall system needed to support scholarship in *this* century, not the 19th century. And all the while we continue to invest and reinvest and increase our investments in the commercial Science, Technology, Engineering & Medicine (STEM) literature that is (by and large) causing the greatest pressure on the system.

But then, the numbers are mind-boggling and can certainly cloud the thinking, and the library community has been very successful in using the drumbeat of price increases to capture the attention of university leaders, which they now have. But those same arguments may not be as effective with faculty—and we may need a new drumbeat. But, I get ahead of myself. Let's return to the plot as it unfolds.

Universities are interesting entities in the system of scholarly communication, representing as they do the entire spectrum of the system: we are the creators, publishers, distributors, consumers, archivists, gatekeepers, and stewards of scholarly works. We understand pieces of the system very well—are expert, in fact—but I do not believe it can be said that we have all the elements acting in concert (not surprisingly, given the nature of the academy).

We haven't yet experienced the "sea change" that seems possible. Or rather, we've been carried along by the tide of commercial interests and haven't been able to galvanize the academic community to consider a new way—a better way—to manage the system.

CHANGES IN USER BEHAVIOR AFFECTING LIBRARIES

In their 2003–2004 report, the Association of Research Libraries (representing 123 research libraries—most of which are associated with a university) reported that circulation and reference transactions have dropped below 1991 levels, but interlibrary loan transactions increased 148 percent in that same period. While there are surely notable exceptions, library users in research universities are visiting the library less frequently, they are checking out fewer items from the local collection, and they are increasing requests for materials not owned by the local library.[2]

Library users are also demonstrating a strong preference for using digital materials—even when those materials are represented in the print collection, and even if they are historical (that is, not current literature). For example, the JSTOR project, which initially digitized 117 older research journal runs in such subject areas as history and economics, found that the print materials were used 692 times during the control period; the digital versions were used almost 12,000 times.

Doubtless there are richer treasure troves of research data to be mined, but even a cursory review seems to indicate that many users use digital content more often than print, and that they have a strong preference for doing so.

Changes in Library Expenditures

In 1990, CIC libraries spent $38 million on serials, and by 2003 serials expenditures in the CIC had risen to $93 million—and 30 percent of that $93 million ($24.3) was spent with three journal publishers: Elsevier, Wiley, and Springer.

And, as library user behavior changes, so do expenditures in research libraries, though in ways that might be surprising. In research libraries, in the last twenty years, overall expenditures for research library services have more than doubled, and expenditures for collections have quadrupled in that period. During that same period the number of staff per student served dropped, and research libraries purchased 17 percent fewer books in 2004 than they did in 1986, but 13 percent more serials.

Buried within this data set is one very startling trend related to the acquisition of electronic resources. In 1994, sixty-three research libraries reported spending just over $11 million on electronic resources. Ten years later, in 2004, one hundred research libraries reported that they were spending almost $270 million on electronic resources. In that same year fourteen of those research libraries reporting indicated that they were spending 50 percent of their collection budget on electronic resources.[2]

Libraries are clearly shifting resources (or acquiring new dollars) to purchase more electronic content—and most particularly serial or journal literature in electronic format from commercial publishers.

CHANGES IN FACULTY BEHAVIOR

By and large, faculty members continue to behave in traditional ways with respect to the published literature. Research demonstrates that they prefer to use electronic resources in their own research, but that they continue to publish in traditional ways (with traditional, print-based publishers).

A Canadian poll surveyed some 696 humanities and social science faculty members at Canadian universities. The results detailed in the study include the following summary:

> The study found that many scholars have become active users of electronic resources in their scholarly research. However, they are still much less likely to try to publish their own scholarship electronically than they are to access materials electronically for scholarly purposes.
>
> The study indicated a number of important reasons for the reticence to publish scholarship electronically. One group of explanations can be referred to as concerns about preservation of scholarship. Respondents indicated that the uncertainty over the long-term availability of electronic resources dampens their enthusiasm towards its use. A second concern is the value (or lack thereof) ascribed to electronic scholarship.... A concern over the perceived value of an electronic publication will inevitably lead to decreased usage of this method of dissemination.[3]

Similarly, Leigh Estabrook conducted a survey of faculty in the CIC universities, in the disciplines of history, anthropology and English. She discovered that the prevailing university and departmental guidelines support the use of digital works in promotion and tenure considerations, and that the definition of scholarship is broadening. However, individual faculty expressed reservations about publishing in electronic format, or creating digital works, because of unclear or confusing information relative to archiving, intellectual property, and access issues. No one, it seems, wishes to be the first to jeopardize his or her promotion.[4]

And, most recently, the Modern Language Association issued a most interesting and comprehensive report on evaluating scholarship for promotion and tenure. Some salient points: (1) demands placed on candidates for publication have been expanding in kind and quantity; (2) the value that departments place on scholarly activity outside the monograph remains within a fairly restricted range; (3) faculty seem to believe that their work will be less valued if published outside the standard publishing paradigm; and (4) norms and expectations of the research university drive behavior in the discipline, with fully 49 percent of all tenure-track faculty members employed in Carnegie doctorate-granting institutions.[5] And the report demonstrates that in fact, faculty appear to be satisfied with the process for promotion and tenure, even though it continues to emphasize publishing models that they profess to find daunting.

But, of course, other disciplines exhibit very different behaviors (mathematics and physics, for example, are disciplines where electronic publishing and particularly pre-print publishing are very much part of their culture).

WHERE WE ARE

Library acquisitions continue to accelerate, with a dramatic increase in the number of electronic resources purchased and available from the commercial sector.

Students and faculty demonstrate strong preference for electronic resources in their research.

Faculty behavior varies by discipline, but the norms and culture are very much embedded in the culture of the discipline under examination. Humanities and social science faculty continue to publish in very traditional ways, while those in physics (for example) are embracing new modes of scholarly communication.

If faculty are in fact beginning to publish in new and different ways should libraries—must they—continue to focus their acquisitions on the commercial sector? Or might they begin to think of these investments in new ways? Ways that support faculty in their efforts to effectively share the results of their scholarship?

So what are we doing in the CIC?

In 2004 and 2005 the provosts of the CIC universities convened a series of summits with deans, librarians, faculty, leaders from the disciplinary societies, and university press directors. These gatherings provided a common base for thinking about the issues.[6] Flowing from that, the provosts recommended action in three areas:

1. Support for Open Access Initiatives

On July 28, 2006, they drafted an open letter to the higher education community that was signed by CIC provosts, as well as provosts from other research universities. The letter read as follows:

> As scholars and university administrators we are acutely aware that the present system of scholarly communication does not always serve the best interests of our institution or the general public. Scholarly publishers, academic libraries, university leaders and schools must themselves engage in an ongoing dialogue about the means of scholarly production and distribution. The dialogue must acknowledge both our competing interests and our common goals. < Open Access > is good for education and good for research. It is good for the American public and it promotes broad, democratic access to knowledge. While it challenges the academy and scholarly publishers to think and act creatively, it need not threaten nor undermine a successful balance of our interests.

2. Promoting a Joint Statement with CIC University Faculty Governance Leaders on Publishing Agreements

The statement, which has been endorsed by the CIC Provosts and is out for a vote in the faculty senates, supports a voluntary agreement that:

Encourages faculty authors to retain non-exclusive rights to their work, including use in their teaching, presentations, and lectures;

Provides for a 6-month embargo, after which the author shall have non-exclusive rights to deposit the work in their home university repository, and on their own Web page;

Encourages the faculty to grant to their institution non-exclusive rights for use of the materials in teaching and other scholarly enterprises on that campus.

The preamble statement expresses the following:

> Publication is the lifeblood of the university. It is incumbent upon faculty, campus administrators and librarians to ensure the free flow of scholarly information in fulfillment of our campus missions to advance the public good through research and education. Toward this end, our campuses are committed to supporting a sustainable publication process and a healthy publishing industry. Suitable publishing printers for academic enterprises should be encouraging the widest possible dissemination of the academy's work, and the management of copyright should be directed to encouraging scholarly output rather than unnecessarily fettering its access and use. Without some important changes in publishing practices, authors and readers will continue to be frustrated by barriers to the free flow of information that is an essential characteristic of great research universities."

3. Establishment of Institutional Repositories

While several CIC universities have launched repositories, the faculty uptake has been relatively slow. Research on institutional repositories suggests that the greatest barriers to deposit seem to be: confusion about intellectual property; onerous submissions processes; and a lack of mandatory submission policies. Conversely, findings suggest that submissions will increase if submission processes are simple, if the process propagates submissions in national or disciplinary repositories, and if indexing in search engines, such as Google, is available.

CIC efforts will look closely at the repositories that have been developed by the member universities. Both Michigan and Illinois have hired staff to work closely with faculty on the submission process, and Purdue has made great progress with faculty on curation and ingestion of data sets. The work will explore two key questions: Do librarian intermediaries make a substantial contribution to the IR development? And to what degree do scholar demographics influence faculty interest and activity in IR development? This effort is funded by Mellon, and it is hoped that the findings will suggest a process for federating these repositories across the CIC and for devising strategies to ensure high faculty participation.

In other action, the CIC university librarians have promulgated a set of guiding principles for mass digitization efforts in the CIC libraries, stating that:

Digitization goals are for wide distribution, improved access methods, preservation of materials, ability to use content in new ways that facilitate new forms of research, ability to leverage the investments of all CIC universities, and avoidance of unnecessary duplication of effort.

Recognizing that standards are dynamic and evolving, the efforts for digitization, access, metadata, storage and preservation will be based on generally accepted and widely adopted international standards.

Resources combined through the federation will be "open access" throughout the CIC to the extent legally permissible, but it is understood that investments will be necessary for the development of the federated resources that might result in charges to users beyond the CIC.

CIC libraries that sign agreements with vendors in order for those vendors to digitize material from library collections agree that such digitization will be done with the intent of encouraging open access and discouraging re-purposing the content for sale by the vendor.

CONCLUSIONS

Perhaps it is not realistic to expect a new and wildly effective system to emerge from the digital community of scholars in the way that YouTube and other services emerged in the social web. But there may be strategies that move us closer to a true community of scholars, engaged and communicating in exciting new ways that are impossible (if not prohibitively costly) in the current environment. Such strategies might include:

1. Engage faculty in the process and target messages to effectively address their concerns and interests. Assurance of an audience for scholarly works may be more compelling, for example, than the economic argument. Look how obsessively the Amazon rankings are pored over—and how people love to Google themselves. How do we build a system that taps into these elements of human behavior?

2. University Presses could be important allies, but here again, the language used, the appeals, and the selection of the messengers will be important.
3. Embolden and prepare administrators to speak up. Experience in the CIC demonstrates that university administrators do wish to provide leadership on these issues, and when they can act together they are emboldened.
4. Support institutional repositories, open access, and digitization efforts—the more ubiquitous digital access the better. And one very specific step for libraries could be to negotiate for rights to have all authors' published works available at the home university.
5. The work of the library to provide coherent access is vitally important. We should continue to release ourselves from the chains of the perfect bibliographic record, and we must focus on simplifying the experience for users of our library Web pages. Some of us have recreated in the virtual world the barriers that exist in the physical world. The average human has a very high tolerance for imprecise research results.
6. Think creatively about repositories as containers for the universe of digital materials produced through research and scholarship, not just the published record. That is, don't segregate information by "type" but rather let the access points filter and display the data as appropriate for the user.

Some of us have been in this business a long while and believe somehow that our very tenure makes us uniquely suited to address these issues, but I fear that actually nothing could be farther from the truth. The human desire for self-protection is extremely difficult to overcome, and while it is useful in helping us imagine how other people and systems should change to be more successful, it prevents us from seeing the problems we ourselves have created and must overcome.

"In the beginner's mind, there are many possibilities. In the expert's mind there are few." Shunryu Suzuki

NOTES

1. *Scholarly Communication: The Report of the National Enquiry* (Baltimore and London: Johns Hopkins University Press, 1979), 30.

2. Kryillidou, Martha and Mark Young, eds. ARL Statistics, 2003–2004, and 2004–2005 (Washington, DC: ARL, 2005 and 2006).

3. Archer, Keith. *Electronic Publishing in the Humanities and Social Sciences: A Report to the Humanities and Social Sciences Federation of Canada on Survey Findings*. 2006. http://www.ourfutureourpast.ca/e-pub/poll/poll.htm, quoted in Frank A. Dominguez, "Establishing the Academic Infrastructure for Scholarly Communication in the Humanities in a Digital World" http://www.unc.edu/scholcomdig/whitepapers/dominguez.pdf..

4. Estabrook, Leigh. "The Book as the Gold Standard for Tenure and Promotion in the Humanistic Disciplines." Committee on Institutional Cooperation. 2003. http://www.cic.uiuc.edu/groups/CIC/archive/Report/ScholarlyCommunicationsSummitReport_Dec03.pdf.

5. Report of the Modern Language Association Task Force on Evaluating Scholarship for Promotion and Tenure. 2007. http://www.mla.org/tenure_promotion

6. The Committee on Institutional Cooperation (CIC) is a consortium of twelve research universities. http://www.cic.uiuc.edu.

A World Infinite and Accessible: Digital Ubiquity, the Adaptable Library, and the End of Information

Dennis Dillon

ABSTRACT. Discusses the four ages of collection development leading up to the "network as library." Information convergence, information ubiquity, and the end of information. Examines the role of the library when there is too much information and the concept of a collection has lost a significant portion of its meaning.

KEYWORDS. Collection development, information convergence, information ubiquity, the network as library

One night a few years ago, I looked over at the bestseller my wife was reading and realized that the redhead on the back cover was my high-school girlfriend.

I readjusted the bedcovers and flipped through the magazine I was reading and, feeling the burden of all the befuddled husbands who had gone before me, asked, "How's the book?"

"It's pretty good," my wife replied, "it's about relationships."

There was that word again, like a recurring nightmare rising up from the swamp of the Lifetime TV network. Now it all came back to me in a flash, the redhead's father had been a psychologist who drove a Plymouth station wagon, the younger brother had tried to punch me out for dating his sister, and the girlfriend in question had done some modeling in New York before becoming a tenured literature professor.

The resulting conversation with my wife went better than expected. "This is her fifth book, it's set in the south, I've read a couple of her others, it's about relationships ... what do you mean ... girlfriend?

All of us have had variations of the resulting conversation. But in a pre-Google world I was blithely unaware that this particular ex-girlfriend had churned out one best seller after another. But of even more critical importance, there was no easy way for the ex to enter into our lives. No search engine was going to bring her face and biography into our living room. Because of this the entire incident became just another minor interlude in the overall thread of our lives. But this husband's pre-Google utopian world of severely limited information is vastly different from the information universe of today.

Several weeks ago I arrived in Mountain View, California in the middle of the night and promptly became utterly lost. In itself this is not a particularly worrying situation, but I needed to pick people up at various mysterious locations the following morning and I also needed to obtain and read critical documents before a 9:00 a.m. meeting. Somehow all the information I needed materialized in the nick of time through Internet and phone connections in a way that no one any longer views as remarkable. The information was literally in the air.

Even the most dimwitted among us have become aware that the very air around us is full of information. Within inches of our heads are countless cell-phone messages, faxes, radio and television signals, wirelessly transmitted Web pages, satellite signals, and the like. With every breath we take, day in and day out, we are inhaling charged electrons carrying potential library shelves worth of digital and analog signals. You can leave your Blackberry at home, but Blackberry signals are wisping through your hair every millisecond of your life. You can't escape information, even if you can't see it. Was that a shiver that just went down your spine, or was it an entry from Wikipedia that your neighbor just pulled up on their cell phone?

In other words, things have changed.

The easy access to music, text, voice, video, and data of all types that is now casually accessed by handheld devices and the widespread availability of information that was once almost impossible to find are the surprise twins of an unexpected revolution. Information convergence and information ubiquity are changing our world. Driven by rapid innovation and worldwide competition, the race to develop the smallest and most powerful communication devices possible, along with the race to develop the most comprehensive and intuitive means of distributing information, are forever changing the comfortable environment in which libraries have existed since the earliest days of the clay tablet and papyrus scroll.

Let's revisit that library history by taking a trip through the four ages of library collection development.

LOOT AND PILLAGE

In the beginning was the age of looting and pillaging. If you saw something you liked you raised an army and went out and took it. This age of collection development lasted from the beginning of the human species until recent times, and the collected loot remains a critical part of the inventory of many of our great museums and libraries. Whether in Roman times or during World War II, collection building by force of arms has been a crucial element in the creation of our understanding of the human historical record. The main problem with this approach has always been the overhead. Raising an army every time you needed something new to read has proved to be an expensive and inefficient way to build a collection.

THE CASTLE

But history moved forward and the development of the printing press and the rise of booksellers changed the traditional collecting dynamic. There were more books to be had and collecting them became a passion with a mystique all its own. Instead of one copy of a book, there were now several hundred, and competing collectors jockeyed to acquire the best collections. The original libraries, built by the privileged and maintained in castles and monasteries, were eventually succeeded by libraries built by universities and municipalities, and thus the local library collection was born. The only problem was again one of overhead. Building castles of books every few miles in order to store a local community's collection was expensive, and there was also a certain lack of choice and control for consumers because they were restricted to whatever books were easily available nearby. You couldn't always get what you wanted, as you could when you had an army at your command, but the general reader did have easier access to more material than ever before.

THE EURAIL PASS

Then came the Internet, which meant that information of every kind poured into homes, schools and coffee shops, and reading peasants no longer had to pay fealty to the local information castle. Libraries adapted to the changed environment by leveraging their budgets and embracing the Eurail-pass style of collection building. With the Eurail Pass style of collecting (also known as licensing) the library never truly owned anything. Just as the real Eurail Pass gave you rights to take a train anywhere (within limits) licensing gave you rights to access information from anywhere (within limits). This cut down on overhead because you no longer needed to raise armies or build castles in order to acquire and store books, but it remained costly because with licensing you still had to pre-pay your access fees, and sometimes life just got in the way and you ended up never using the information you paid for (or in the case of the real Eurail pass—never taking the train at all). The Eurail-pass style of collecting also led to a further loss of control for librarians, since information was sold in bundles containing bits and pieces the library didn't want, while other features that the library did want were simply not available—but for the reader this was once again an improvement because they had easier access to more material than ever before.

THE NETWORK AS LIBRARY

With every passing age of collection development there is more information, and this information is cheaper and easier to get to, and there is less need for a single authority to control it, whether that central authority happens to be armies, castle guards, or gate-keeping librarians. This brings us to the fourth age of collection development: the network as library. In this age the cost of the local collection overhead is reduced even further, but so is the control of the librarian authority figure, and to continue the trend, the reader also has easier access to more information than ever before. The network as library is composed of an almost limitless amount of instantaneously available content. Information bottlenecks continue to exist with licensed content and with content still locked up in print, but mass digitization efforts, pay-per-view, the open access movement, and changing business models are increasingly attempting to transform these information legacies and make them part of the more seamless and accessible worldwide networked library.

But when the network becomes the library, the concept of a library collection loses a significant portion of its meaning. An effective collection can no longer be purchased or licensed because information is globally dispersed and constantly changing. The very organization of information is different and more complex. Network-based information is more fluid and is increasingly more collaborative in nature, it may not have easily identifiable authors, it may be organized by social networks or computer algorithms, it is more open to ongoing user inputs, creativity, and innovation; and it is taking on a different structure than the more static constructions of the book and journal that were born of the limitations of the printing press. In other words, even the largest library collections may soon be no more than somewhat pale and limited imitations of what is easily available on the network.

When the New Yorker runs a story that casually mentions Google's intent to digitize everything in OCLC WorldCat, that is a wake-up call.[1] When this happens just two weeks after the reality television show "Beauty and the Geek" features an elimination segment in which the college graduate contestants are forced to attempt what is considered the almost Herculean task of locating a static book on a non-dynamic library shelf using the Dewey Decimal system, then librarians might wonder if we aren't increasingly viewed as somewhat humorous guardians from the past, destined to serve the old, the clueless, the academic, and the oddly out of touch.

INFORMATION MONOPOLY

Up until fifteen years ago, libraries had a comfortable information monopoly. Libraries were in every university and every town in America. If you wanted authoritative information you had little choice but to go to the library. We were both the Rockefellers and the Microsoft of information. And then, almost before we could even form a committee to discuss the issue, we not only lost that monopoly, but became somewhat bemused bystanders as innovators poured out of every nook and cranny with new ways to find and use information. These efforts emerged from an entirely different value system, and have ranged from the Internet-based iTunes music library to the video libraries of YouTube and Yahoo, to the routine creation of content and the uploading of files by millions of MySpace users, to Google's dalliance with digitizing the contents of the world's major traditional libraries, to the collaborative creativity of the multilingual worldwide interactive encyclopedia, Wikipedia. What happened? iTunes, YouTube, MySpace, Wikipedia, and Google Books are successfully used by millions of people every day without any librarian help. Somehow, as well-organized librarians held conferences, discussed issues on listservs, published articles, developed standards, attended meetings, and transformed library spaces—the arc of history passed over our heads both unnoticed and un-acted upon.

MOSAIC

In the winter of 1993 a handful of library staff assembled in a small office to await the release of some new software on an Illinois FTP site. The minute it was released the software was downloaded and installed and suddenly the computer came to life with text and images and also with the voice of Marc Andreessen welcoming the group to use the newly downloaded tool, named NCSA Mosaic, to explore the World Wide Web. Everyone in that room knew in an instant that the world of libraries had changed forever. Pandora's Box had been opened and all of us there at the time understood that there was no way to lure the suddenly loosed Web demons back to where they came from. Within months several colleagues had quit to pursue Internet opportunities, and they never returned. The instantly obvious vision of an Internet full of online books, journals, and movies, and with everything either in the public domain or available on a pay-per-view or advertising supported basis, has changed little since. What was not foreseen, however, was the growth of the open source movement, the rise of collaborative communities, the increase of new arenas for creativity, and the changes and impacts that information fluidity and the unleashing of more dynamic methods of communicating, sharing knowledge, discovering the works of others, and the effects that the minute by minute compiling of human knowledge would have on society.

THE END OF INFORMATION

None of us knows what will come next, but for libraries it is not unreasonable to assume that it is the end of information as we know it. If information *is* what information professionals *do*, in an age of information ubiquity, who is it that will need information professionals? If information itself changes and continues to shed its static and non-dynamic components, how will libraries adapt? Libraries have always saved and collected information in the belief that the most valuable information occurs in discrete collectable units. But with the advent of the Web, libraries did not rush to collect Web pages and other related dynamic information, precisely because they were not unchanging and they were not published in the traditional manner. The New York Times Web page changes every few minutes throughout the day, and the fact that libraries don't collect it would seem to indicate that it has no value—but we all know that this is not true. Libraries know how to deal with information formats from the seventeenth century, but we do not know how to deal effectively with today's information. But this is not the only issue with the nature of twenty-first-century information. Just as every fish is reasonably competent and knowledgeable about the changing currents, temperature, and chemical make-up of water they live in, when easy access to information is part of our everyday environment, suddenly all of us find ourselves immersed in the information water and everyone of us is reasonably competent, knowledgeable, and confident using tools that were once confined to information professionals. What reference librarian of twenty years ago could compete with a high-school student of today armed with Google, Google Scholar, Google Books, and Wikipedia—not to mention hundreds of other similar information tools. The universe of information defined by the library monopoly of the recent past is disappearing and it is not coming back.

Many of us worry that our industry is in danger of becoming the latest victim of technological progress just as other previous labor-intensive handcraft efforts similar to libraries were eliminated by the industrial revolution. Just as the technology of the spinster and the spinning wheel suddenly had to compete against the new automated factories, the technology of the book on the library shelf is now competing against interactive electronic Web pages. Librarians' love affair with specialized information gathering and information fragmentation in the form of branch libraries, special collections, special shelving locations, hundreds of different databases on every topic imaginable, carefully selected purchases of individual books, and peculiar localized solutions and projects for every possible user segment, is running up against an alternative world view that attempts to make all information efficiently and easily accessible through one interface and one device. Arcane knowledge of which special shelf a book might be on, or the library spelling of a name everyone else spells differently, is no longer critical for an audience that increasingly has other options.

What is frightening is how fast things have changed. The Occupational Outlook Handbooks from the mid-1980s forecast a solid job market for telephone operators throughout the 1990s. Yet nowadays they are called communication equipment operators and the job prospects are less than rosy. The need for people who specialize in connecting users over this particular network has been all but automated out of existence. Other intermediary information industries from newspapers to travel agents and television networks are facing similar distress. And how many telephone operators would have guessed that by 2007 the biggest manufacturers of cameras would be the telephone companies? Information convergence and information ubiquity are traveling hand-in-hand in a race that seems focused on the goal of becoming ever smaller and faster: smaller and faster devices, smaller and faster search results, and inevitably smaller, faster and more nimble organizations.

GOOGLE

In recent question-and-answer sessions about the Google library project, librarians and faculty have expressed concern about the process of selecting items for Google Books. The expectation that the effectiveness of the project depends on the careful selection of materials by librarians runs directly counter to Google's world view that their database will simply include all information, and that users are perfectly capable of selecting their own information for their own use, just as they currently select their own doctors, spouses, houses, food, and investments. These two viewpoints represent radically different ways of approaching information. One springs from an age of information scarcity in which every book and journal was a precious object and needed to be selected by an expert, and the other from an age of information ubiquity that says "let's throw all the information into one big pile and let computer algorithms and users figure it out on their own."

In one sense, the paragraphs above overstate the dangers currently faced by libraries. It took a generation for cars to replace horses or for the telephone to replace the telegraph, and libraries, even more than these examples, are firmly embedded social constructs that do more than serve as merely economically efficient information middlemen. Use of libraries has grown dramatically over the last five decades and libraries have done a remarkable job of embracing new technology and staying relevant, frequently leading the technological way on their campuses and in their communities. There is some content that, for various reasons, is unlikely to ever be online. But in a "what have you done for me lately" world, libraries still have to compete for scarce funds in an environment that is sprouting information competitors at a phenomenal rate, competitors who have a different concept of what information is, and a different concept of how to connect and interact with users.

WHAT IS INFORMATION?

What is clear is that in the information world, libraries are no longer the big fish in a small pond, but are instead small fish in a rapidly expanding pond, and adapting to being a small fish requires a radically different set of skills. For one thing, small fish need to be quicker. It is also now abundantly clear that the library view of how to most effectively handle information is not the only view.

Librarians are information professionals, but I've never met a thoughtful librarian who professed to know what information is. The information we deal with: books, journals, databases, maps, manuscripts, recorded music, and so on, is clearly information, but so are the songs on iTunes, the video clips on YouTube, the minute-by-minute changing entries on Wikipedia, and the data from an ocean buoy, a pixel from a digital image, or a DNA gene sequence. One useful definition may be that information is *anything that is capable of producing a reaction in the human brain or change in the human mind*. For many librarians of today this type of discussion is viewed as just useless philosophical hogwash, but for the information professionals graduating twelve months from now who will be assisting users in finding their way around the rapidly mutating global network, or managing data streams from Afghani radio and deep-space satellites, this wider more inclusive concept of information will be their job.

It's not about information; it's about what you do with it.

As librarians we have tended to believe that in the end, it really is all about the information. This is partly because of our philosophical belief in privacy, which has always meant that we helped people locate the information they needed, and then we essentially vanished, treating the information request as a one-time event, and not as a possible life-long interest. We have always been careful not to pry too deeply into our customer's motivations or their intended use of the information we provide. But maybe it is really not just about the information, anymore than the local iceman who delivered ice for old-fashioned refrigerators was just about the ice, or the old local stables were about the horse, or the telephone was about the handset at the end of the landline, or the map was about the paper it was printed on. In today's world anyone can get information. It's not just about information, it's about what you do with it, and doing more with information is the basis for the rapidly mutating innovations known as Web 2.0 that are raising the information bar to even newer heights. Just as we think we understand what information users want, they mystify and tantalize us with even more ideas about what their information tools could do for them. For librarians it may be about information, but for users it may be about creativity, or changing lives, or producing events, or connections, or products that transform society; it may be about using information in a collaborative way to multiply and expand its value, and to do this, users need the library to, at least, not prevent or hinder their ability to use and re-use information in creative and flexible ways.

So what are the possible library reactions to a world of information ubiquity? Let me mention two: one is somewhat cynical and the other is essentially unfathomable. The first lies in deciphering the lessons in human behavior that can be gleaned from the sale of bottled water.

BOTTLED WATER

How can librarians compete in a leveled playing field where we no longer have the innate advantage previously provided by our inside knowledge of the library and its obscure Byzantine rules, bureaucracies, and interesting personalities? For a clue we can try to decipher how the American business community has found a way to make money off of one of the most ubiquitous commodities on Earth—water. In the United States water is plentiful, cheap, and safe, and yet an entire industry has grown up in recent years selling for dollars what people can easily get for pennies. The number one brand of bottled water in the country, Aquafina, comes from, among other places, the municipal water supply of Wichita, Kansas and yet the citizens of Wichita happily pay a fortune to Aquafina to buy their tap water at a corner store in a plastic bottle. Dasani, the number two bottled water brand, comes from the tap water of Queens, New York and Jacksonville, Florida and likewise the citizens of these municipalities happily pay dearly for the privilege of drinking their own tap water out of an expensive container infused with plastic molecules, containers that environmentalists consider an unmitigated landfill and petrochemical disaster.

Historical testaments like these to the triumph of marketing over what would appear to be common sense are almost infinite. The point being that marketing geniuses have developed means for tapping complex human motivations, weaknesses, and desires to the extent that they are able to persuade people to pay more money per cubic foot for bottled water than people pay for the very houses they live in. There is a lesson to be learned here. Just because something is ubiquitous and essentially free, does not mean that people are unwilling to pay for perceived added value and convenience. Librarians already have a respected brand name, and an argument can be made that all we may need to do to ensure our continued survival is to provide effective information packaging, add value and convenience, and market ourselves more effectively.

THE INTELLIGENCE COMMUNITY

A second possible library response to information ubiquity is contained in the gathering insights that are coming out of the intelligence community as they recast their purpose from the secrets business to the information business. This reinvention is not surprising since in a single day they handle a volume of the world's e-mail, telephone conversations, and faxes that dwarf the contents of a large research library. In today's world intelligence analysts find that they often have too much information. The decisions involving Iraq have been cited as a classic case of too much information. Iraq's history and internal divisions have long been well documented in every major library in the world. In the pre-war discussions the world was awash with information, commentary, and experts, and yet all of that information eventually led to a state of affairs that virtually no one is happy with.

National security expert Gregory Treverton has talked about information overload issues like Iraq as being in a problem class that he calls "mysteries." "Mysteries require judgments and the assessment of uncertainty, and the hard part is not that we have too little information, but that we have too much."[2]

As librarians we want to believe that adding to the volume of information can improve the outcome of a decision-making process, but the evidence for this is dubious. Does having more information make it any easier to predict who will win a football game? Does having more information about healthcare options, or even what food we should eat, make national or even specific personal decisions, any easier or wiser? We can all agree that better analysis of the information we have, analysis by more thoughtful people with greater analytical skills and more experience can help. But with mysteries we aren't always smart about handling the information we do have, which is precisely why they are mysteries. Surveys and polls early in the Iraq debate were clear about how the collective wisdom of the crowds viewed the situation, with every major poll showing that more than 70 percent of Americans approved of the decision to go to war.[3] There was plenty of information, and there was plenty of crowd-based wisdom; what was missing was judgment. What was missing was the ability of decision makers to make effective use of the information they had. It's not about information, it's about what you do with it. What was missing were the voices of Sam Spade, Perry Mason, Miss Marple, and other experienced and perceptive interpreters of the infinitude of human nature, people who were possessed of the ability to dispassionately dissect the situation, untangle the mystery, and render reasoned judgment.

One of the key concepts in communications theory is that it is important to reduce the amount of noise in any given signal. In order to better understand what is being said on radio or the TV, engineers work constantly to improve the strength and clarity of the signal and to reduce the amount of distracting static and background noise. In written communications editors perform the same function, reducing the clutter and static of the author's drafts in order to produce a focused, clear narrative. In search retrieval, the traditional goal has always been to design a system that retrieves a maximum amount of relevant information with a minimum amount of static and noise. The goal of any information organization is to produce a clear signal with a minimal amount of noise.

Libraries want to make it easy for users to get what they need with the fewest number of clicks and a minimal amount of intervening distractions, all while knowing that if we don't or can't do this effectively, others will. No one can untangle a mystery if they aren't able to understand the signal. So what is the library's noise-to-signal ratio? Do we have one clear search box for all our resources? Do we provide complete Web 2.0 functionality for all our resources? Are all of our library's resources findable through Google? Can both a beauty and a geek use the library without specialized training? If the answer to any of these questions is no, then we have to ask ourselves—are we truly making a serious attempt to reduce the amount of library-generated noise and static? Why is this even a question? Possibly because we are, in some sense, our own worst enemy. Libraries receive noise and signals both, and we send noise and signals both. It is the library culture to be extremely receptive to all the input we receive and to provide what information we do have without filters and without massaging. We listen and attempt to respond to every individual user, every individual need, and every opinion. One of the choices we face in an information world that is infinite and accessible, is whether to define all the input our libraries receive as legitimate signals, or to consider exercising judgment and defining some of it as noise and static, and then dealing with it accordingly. Historically we have played a largely passive role. We listened to what people wanted, we bought what publishers offered, and we presented our collections—the library signal—in a largely minimalist and passive manner. We did not attempt to proactively shape or filter the information environment around us, or exert ourselves to distinguish between noise and signal. We were neutral channels through which information flowed. What we mostly did was shop. We shopped for books, we shopped for vendor-supplied software systems, and we shopped for places to hold conferences where we then discussed how and where to shop. We also created a culture where sitting around talking about shopping was considered work. What we don't talk about is whether this is what we should be doing, or how long our funding institutions will consider this type of activity to be a good return on their investment.

Historically, our users have indicated in a general way what they are interested in, and we have then gone out and shopped on their behalf, purchasing gifts that we hoped they would appreciate such as new books, databases, and e-journals in fields where they have indicated past interest. We have then scattered these gifts across our library shelves and Web pages, and later helped users figure out where we put them. This entire library operational structure is in some danger as users begin to shop for themselves, and as tools are developed to help users effectively locate what they want on their own, and as vendors emerge to supply the items users want.

The ability to distinguish between noise and signal is essentially another way of describing a process of routinely making the distinctions that can lead to effective decisions. Lurking underneath this discussion about noise and signal is a question about the future direction of libraries. Bending over backwards to respond to every single user no matter what they want can be considered good customer service by an organization that is both able and willing to respond to every need. On the other hand it can be considered a disservice to the mass of an organization's users if the organization's talent and resources are not devotedly developing proactive strategies to improve its central signal, but are instead being consumed by responding to what are essentially the minor cracks and pops that make up the static on the channel.

Recently a group of senior librarians gathered for a day-long meeting to think about big issues. The hotel was sponsoring two conferences that day and due to some karmic convergence, the conference next door was devoted to endangered species. For librarians it wasn't always clear whether we were in the right breakout rooms or not, but one of these breakout sessions was unmistakably entitled, "The Network as the Library." The starting point for this breakout discussion was: if the network is destined to be the mega library to end all libraries—what will our role be?

Beginning with a scenario where Google has more books than the Library of Congress, and where publishers are offering easy pay-per-view access to in-copyright material, the assembled librarians discussed five future roles for librarians:

1. a fiscal role in which libraries continue to be the funding sources for library users accessing licensed or pay-per-view content;
2. an access role, where the library provides specialized access tools to certain types of material;
3. a niche collection role, where the libraries collect certain types of material for their user group that will not easily be available otherwise;
4. a niche service role, where the library provides special personalized information services to its user group; and
5. a preservation role, for those items that are worth preserving and are otherwise at risk.

These five roles, when paired with effective marketing and the expertise to at least aid in the discovery and manipulation of Web 2.0-enabled information needed to solve mysteries, could ensure a valued future for any library adapting to an information world that is infinite and accessible.

ANTOINE DE SAINT-EXUPÉRY

The early twentieth-century French aviator, Antoine de Saint-Exupéry, had another perspective. He said: "If you want to build a ship, don't drum up men to gather wood, divide the work and give orders. Instead teach them to yearn for the vast and endless sea."[4] The Web has already taught people to want this vast and endless sea of information, and they are already building the ships. Every day brings new Internet tools for finding and sharing information. Millions of people who haven't been in a library in years, are now busy helping to build what is, in essence, the new global networked library. We suddenly have millions of new colleagues and this can only be good. It also shifts the meaning of what it is to be a librarian.

If on the network everyone can be a publisher, everyone can organize content, everyone can help make things findable through the magic of Web 2.0, and everyone can archive and migrate content—then we all win. If Exupéry is right and we don't have to "divide up all the work and give all the orders," then librarians can do something else more fruitful with our time. It means that both my ex-girlfriend and wife were probably right, it is somehow probably about relationships, new relationships both personal and technical that haven't yet been fully developed, but it is also very much about being able to stand back and exercise perspective and judgment. If people are suddenly yearning for a "vast and endless sea" it means that our task as librarians is to re-imagine our jobs in a world where information skills are widely dispersed, a world where we are no longer the only information experts. It means that we have to think differently, connect differently, become smaller and faster, reduce the noise-to-signal ratio, and learn to use the ships that others are building—and on occasion learn how to build better ships ourselves. More tools being used by more people can only make our jobs more interesting. When the Web is the library, we're all librarians, and that is an interesting world.

NOTES

1. Toobin, Jeffrey, "Google's Moon Shot," *New Yorker*, February 5, 2007, 30–35.
2. Gladwell, Malcolm. "Open Secrets," *New Yorker*, January 8, 2007, 44–53.
3. Iraq, Polling Report, http://www.pollingreport.com/iraq.htm.
4. Quoted from Exupéry's *Wisdom of the Sands* in "Mr. Green," by Elizabeth Kolbert, *New Yorker*, January 22, 2007, 39.

Social, Intellectual, and Cultural Spaces: Creating Compelling Library Environments for the Digital Age

Barbara I. Dewey

ABSTRACT. Transformation of research library space to address the changing environment of scholarship, teaching, and learning is a common occurrence. The transformations are a result of the migration from print to digital, the opportunity to leverage campus partnerships, and adoption of more user-centered approaches for space planning. This paper will explore a collaborative transformation process for creating new physical and virtual spaces to support the changing needs of twenty-first-century students and scholars.

KEYWORDS. Information Commons, partnerships user-centered, collaborative, transformation, spaces

INTRODUCTION

Library space transformation is exploding across colleges and universities today. This paper will explore a collaborative transformation process for creating new spaces to support the changing needs of twenty-first-century students and scholars. We librarians want to connect with them in as many ways as possible and encourage them to connect with each other in new ways supported by new technology. The development process for creating the University of Tennessee Libraries' Commons will be used as an example. This newly created, service-intensive space is a partnership with the Office of Information Technology (OIT) and several colleges. The Commons is based on the "circle of service" model and embraces the notion of connecting students to the information, assistance, and services they need to be successful. I will discuss the importance of library as intellectual, social, and cultural space in the physical and virtual sense and explore selected examples of emerging "new" spaces that connect students and/or faculty to collections and services in innovative and effective ways. Indicators of success and next steps for library transformation in the digital age will conclude the paper.

SCENARIO FOR CHANGE

The current wave of library transformations is based on many factors. The digital revolution in its broadest sense is, I believe, the primary driver. Students, in particular, are living in the digital world, socially and intellectually. Libraries are developing and purchasing digital collections and databases, as well as services to help people access digital resources. At least we are in the same general digital space with our users—or are we? If we, as educators, truly believe that our expensive collections and numerous services are relevant and vital to the intellectual development of students and the process of creating knowledge, we must do everything we can to be in the same space. Students or faculty should be co-creators of new spaces to ensure relevance and usability. Specific environmental factors illustrating the imperative to change and transform include:

The changing nature of libraries and the need to repurpose spaces built for the print era;

Student and faculty reliance on digital scholarship and its supporting technology;

The need to create effective learning spaces and services for "Net-gen" students;

Attracting and retaining the best and brightest students who have choices;

The desire to access, "remix," and share digital resources and rich media in new ways; and

Addressing the imperative for "always on" 24/7 services, collections, and environments.[1]

Accessing, creating, and supporting digital content in all of its manifestations in a dynamic environment drives both physical and virtual changes. New spaces should immerse students' scholarly digital content and connect them with supporting expertise and services.

EMERGING FROM THE UNIVERSITY LIBRARIES' TRANSFORMATION PROCESS

The Commons, located in the University of Tennessee Hodges Library[2] came out of a larger library transformation process to strategically address our services, collections, and spaces to meet the needs of twenty-first-century students and faculty for a campus of 27,000 students, 1,350 faculty, and 6,900 staff. Hodges Library, a relatively new facility, opened in 1987. Well known for innovative application of technology and strong service orientation, we were nonetheless increasingly confined and constrained by space configuration in a 1980s building. Although occasionally overlapping and connecting, we were in a different time and space than our "born digital" students and next generation faculty. We also had to consider how we were going to transform nineteenth-century practices, and reallocate staff and spaces to strengthen our relevance and connections. Study groups were developed around six areas we knew were changing radically, especially because of digitally based factors—more digital, less print collections, students bypassing library resources altogether, and faculty using our virtual space more than our physical space. The six study groups dealt with:

Services and spaces;
Digital production;
Access to content—user interfaces/user awareness;
Periodicals management;
Collection management/technical processes; and
Special collections and archives.

The transformation process is ongoing. Key outcomes to date include merging Special Collections and the Digital Library Center to operationalize digitization of our unique collections and develop the Digital Production Unit (to replace traditional Reserves), and begin to support our emerging institutional repository.

SERVICES AND SPACES STUDY GROUP RECOMMENDATIONS

The Services and Spaces Study Group charge was to conduct an analysis of Hodges Library public service points in terms of the needs of twenty-first-century users and the most effective use of human resources and space. The report proved to be our transformational breakthrough. The group's work centered on answering the question of how to make a 1987 library building more relevant, functional, and user friendly. When it opened, the building featured "wow factor" grand marble staircases, huge hallways, and spacious atria. Service desks were numerous but invisible from the massive hallways. Large areas, such as the Reserve Book Room and the Periodicals Room, needed repurposing since these collections are now largely digital. Additionally, the library had experienced positive collaborations with the Office of Information Technology (OIT) through creation of the Digital Media Service,[3] a drop-off production facility to digitize faculty course-related materials in all formats, implementation of VolPrint,[4] a system of pay-for-print, and development of innovative strategies for integrating scholarly resources and library services within the University's course management system (Online@UT) using The Teaching Library@UT Web site and the virtual reference Web site AskUs.Now.[5] Additional collaborations with OIT were needed and desirable.

THE COMMONS

Recognizing the implications of the new digital context, as well as the key characteristics of net-generation students and faculty, the Services and Spaces Study Group recommended that an information commons be developed in partnership with OIT in the high profile space occupied by the Reserve Book Room (7,788 sq. ft.) and extending throughout the entire second floor (47,000 sq. ft.). A ground floor computer lab operated by OIT would be absorbed in the Commons. Complimentary services and spaces already existed on this heavily used floor including a 24-hour Starbucks Cyber café, The Studio[6] (a multimedia authoring and production lab), and the Welcome Center, containing the main entrance to the library and the circulation desk. Other recommendations included moving periodicals and microforms to the first floor enabling the information commons to encompass the entire floor. Further phases would include renovation of the Media Services area to expand multimedia computing and other technologically and media-rich user space.

An information commons steering committee was formed and in April 2005. Joan Lippincott, Associate Executive Director, Coalition for Networked Information, spent the day with staff from the library and OIT presenting on collaborative learning space development and advising on important aspects of implementation. Members of the committee included the library associate dean (as facilitator); assistant dean of libraries and head, media services; dean of libraries; CIO; head of reference and instructional services; manager of OIT customer support; executive director of OIT customer support; system administrator, OIT Labs, Coordinator, OIT educational technology, electronic services librarian; coordinator of library instructional services; library Web designer, manager of OIT customer support; head, digital media service; and manager of OIT customer technical support. An ambitious opening of mid-August 2005 of the initial phase of what was now to be called "The Commons" opened in August 2005, a mere six months from its conception.

Key components of early planning included creation of a vision for the facility as well as guided principles for planning. The vision: The Commons is a collaborative partnership between the Office of Information Technology and the University Libraries to connect students and faculty with the tools and information they need to be successful learners and teachers in the twenty-first century. Guiding principles for The Commons were formulated and continue to be valuable as we develop new services and renovate additional areas. The principles keep planners on track and disciplined to remain focused on the users' perspective.

The Commons:

Is a true partnership of the Libraries and OIT;
Is a physical and virtual environment;
Leverages joint expertise of Libraries/OIT faculty and staff;
Focuses on the needs of undergraduates (but also serves graduates and faculty);
Will increase services, access to content, and technology for users;
Will be a 24/7 environment;
Will be developed in a phased approach;
Will be flexible, innovative, and appealing;
Will be developed with advice from students and other key campus groups.

The Commons featured the "circle of service" philosophy incorporating the "one-stop shopping around the clock" imperative. Initial services in phase one included information/reference, laptop checkout, technical assistance with logins, 24-hour book retrieval from the stacks, printing/copying/scanning, statistical consulting, wireless access, Digital Media Service pick-up point, presentation practice room, and computer technical support. All funding came from within the library and the OIT budgets, and staffing from reallocation and/or relocation of existing library/OIT positions.

Proof of Concept Budgetary Strategy

The Dean of Libraries and the Chief Information Officer, OIT, forged a strong partnership each bringing to the table a set of human and other resources needed to bootstrap development of the Commons. Jointly we presented the Commons "circle of service" concept to the Chancellor characterizing the project as high impact and critical for student success. We used a phased approach to discuss funding strategies. We proposed funding from three sources—the Chancellor, Libraries, and OIT. Graphical representations helped make the pitch even though we were unsure of the cost in future phases. Statistics demonstrating phase one usage further supported the case for significant investment in the Commons.

Creating the Buzz

The Dean of Libraries and CIO wanted to create additional support for the Commons and gave presentations to the Deans and the Vice Chancellors early in the fall semester right after phase one opened. More presentations were given to student groups and committees encouraging students to let their peers know of the new services and obtain feedback on how the Commons was working for them. Students continue to provide valuable advice for space and service adjustments. The presentations helped create support and excitement. A loud and distinctive "buzz" was created, combined with publicity generated by the Commons public relations subgroup in the form of news releases, a Web site, and large banners describing the Commons. The marketing plan at this stage was modest and pointed—Computer Help, Research Assistance, Fully Loaded Computers—but it worked. Students immediately embraced the facility.

Early Indicators of Success

Indicators of success included dramatic increases in gate count (December 2005 gate count was up 46 percent from December 2004), circulation (up 79 percent), and room count (over 400 students midweek at midnight in the Commons). The student perspective is well represented by two quotes. Kristen, a sports management student, noted that "every time I have been in the library after hours, the Commons has been packed full of students. Some students were finishing assignments, some were doing group projects, and some were just relaxing with friends. The group study areas are of the perfect number and size, and the computers have all the programs I could need on them. I cannot wait until the whole Commons project is complete." Mark, a business major adds, "The Commons is a great addition to the library. Students can study in groups or study alone, check our laptops, use computers, get help and find all the information they need in one room. The Commons has become the one stop shop at the library making it user friendly."

THE COMMONS—PHASE TWO

The Commons, phase one, was initially developed without additional funding or professional designers but through reallocations, modest one-time investments, and existing furnishings. Now that the proof of concept was visible, the Dean of Libraries and CIO secured funding from the Chancellor and Vice Chancellors to expand the Commons into the Periodicals Room (10,171 square feet). Designers were hired to develop plans and a more accurate budget estimate for the expanded Commons. An ambitious design resulted, incorporating flexible furnishings for group and individual work, counters and stools for quick e-mail, soft furnishings for more comfortable study and collaboration, and areas for tutorial and instructional purposes. Renovations and additional furnishings are in progress at this writing but new services were immediately added to the expanded space (once all of the periodicals and microforms were relocated to storage or the first floor). The OIT help desk, computer triage service, expanded laptop checkout, newly configured information/research service area, mobile audio/video conferencing services, additional presentation and group work rooms, and tutoring services were installed and ready for fall semester 2006. The "circle of service" expanded and partnerships increased.

The Commons as a Social/Cultural Space

Providing appealing social spaces and opportunities for refreshment in a 24-hour mode was an important goal even before the Commons was developed. Aramark Food Services installed a Starbucks Café in 2001 on the second floor of Hodges Library adjacent to a small convenience store developed earlier. It was the first Starbucks franchise in Knoxville,

Tennessee and one of only a few 24-hour coffee installations. Starbucks was an immediate, if not resounding, success and provided appealing social spaces for students and faculty to meet, and also provided a safe venue for late-night snacking without going outside. A study area behind the coffee shop was developed into a Cyber café with walk-up workstations to check e-mail or surf the Net. Now, reconfiguration of these spaces as part of the Commons is in the planning stages. Also included are the main entrance, or what has been called the Welcome Center (which was not very welcoming in its original form), and the Mary E. Greer Room, formerly a little used faculty lounge. The design intends to provide additional comfortable, group friendly, and individual seating featuring a proposed media wall to draw people into the library. The Greer Room, an enclosed space, will be a flexibly furnished multipurpose space for cultural events, receptions, seminars, and study when not otherwise in use.

THE COMMONS—PHASE THREE

A third phase of the Commons is planned for the current Media Services and Studio area, a large (7,033 sq. ft.) but underutilized space. The Studio opened in 2001. It provides a place, the expertise, and the technologies for students and faculty to combine digital media in creative ways. The Studio is extremely popular and needs additional space. The remainder of the space, Media Services, is currently occupied by many individual viewing carrels that are not used to capacity. The steering committee is working on a plan to:

Expand the facilities infrastructure to support Studio improvements;
Provide 24-hour access to multifunctional computers (media and productivity);
Create a single primary service point in the room;
Use OIT Student Technology Assistants for Research and Teaching (START) to train users and reserve presentation practice rooms;
Consider alternative locations for Studio Mac-based instruction;
Consider a "genius bar/technology showcase" installation;
Incorporate media wall; and
Expand partnerships with OIT by collaborating on equipment purchase, software upgrades, technical support, assistance with media conversion, and delivery of campus TV feed to Hodges Library.

The designers, in working on phase three plans, are asked to preserve as many enclosed rooms as possible for production purposes, ensure that staff spaces and media collections are secure, and remove walls to further integrate the space with the rest of the Commons.

Research and Inspiring Spaces

The Commons is an ideal spot for undergraduates to gather, work, socialize, and be alone in a crowd. However, we hear, especially from graduate students and faculty, about the need for quiet, inspiring study spaces. A growing number of research libraries have developed or are planning physical and virtual library spaces especially for graduate students and/or faculty. Examples include research commons, reading rooms, labs, and spaces for collaborative as well as virtual research and collaborative spaces. Other libraries have renovated grand, historic spaces specifically for quiet, contemplative study. The University of Tennessee has a 75-year-old library building, Hoskins Library, in desperate need of renovation. We are exploring designating it as a humanities center with research space contiguous with a grand reading room, the Digital Library Center,[7] and Special Collections.[8] Boston College,[9] University of Southern California,[10] and University of Oklahoma[11] have recently transformed similar era buildings featuring inspiring reading rooms meant for quiet study.

Next Steps in Spaces Development

Creating spaces for advancing intellectual, social, and cultural development in the digital era includes exploring new possibilities for virtual spaces. We are in the process of developing a robust virtual Commons.[12] Other universities such as Vassar,[13] University of Michigan,[14] and Washington University[15] have developed virtual collaboration spaces for faculty as well. University of Minnesota[16] and North Carolina State University[17] libraries feature integrated social communication spaces as part of their services. Extending the "circle of service" concept to the rest of the campus advances universities' goals of integrating expertise, technology, and environments that are needed to support teaching, learning, and the creation of new knowledge. Extending the circle of service further underscores student- and faculty-centered strategies for immersing the campus in digital scholarship, twenty-first-century communication options, and richer interdisciplinary collaborations.

NOTES

1. Lippincott, Joan K. "Net Generation Students & Libraries," EDUCAUSE Review (March/April 2005): 56-66.
2. The Commons, University of Tennessee Libraries and Office of Information Technology (OIT), http://commons.utk.edu/ (accessed February 21, 2007).
3. Digital Media Service, http://digitalmedia.utk.edu/ (accessed February 21, 2007).
4. VolPrint, University of Tennessee, http://volprint.utk.edu/ (accessed February 21, 2007).
5. AskUs.Now, http://www.lib.utk.edu/refs/askusnow/ (accessed February 21, 2007).
6. The Studio, University of Tennessee Libraries, http://www.lib.utk.edu/mediacenter/studio/index.html (accessed February 21, 2007).
7. University of Tennessee Libraries. Digital Library Center, http://diglib.lib.utk.edu/cgi/b/bib/bib-idx (accessed February 21, 2007).
8. University of Tennessee. Special Collections Department, http://www.lib.utk.edu/spcoll/ (accessed February 21, 2007).
9. Boston College. Babst Library, http://www.bc.edu/libraries/centers/bapst/ (accessed February 21, 2007).
10. University of Southern California. Doheny Memorial Library, http://www.usc.edu/libraries/locations/doheny/ (accessed February 21, 2007).
11. University of Oklahoma Libraries. Bizzell Memorial Library, http://libraries.ou.edu/ (accessed February 21, 2007).
12. University of Tennessee Libraries and OIT Commons, http://commons.utk.edu/ (accessed February 21, 2007).
13. Vassar College Media Cloisters, http://mediacloisters.vassar.edu/ (accessed February 21, 2007).
14. University of Michigan Libraries. Faculty Exploratory, http://www.lib.umich.edu/exploratory/ (accessed February 21, 2007).
15. Washington University Olin Library. Washington University Digital Gateway, http://www.lib.umich.edu/exploratory/ (accessed February 21, 2007).
16. University of Minnesota Libraries. UThink: Blogs at the University of Minnesota, http://blog.lib.umn.edu/ (accessed February 21, 2007).
17. North Carolina State University Libraries. WolfWikis and WolfBlogs, http://www.lib.ncsu.edu/community/ (accessed February 21, 2007).

A Question of Access—
Evolving Policies and Practices

Heather Joseph

ABSTRACT. As scholarship becomes ever more digitally driven, the communication of peer-reviewed research results has undergone a dramatic transformation. The Internet has created an unprecedented environment where these results can be immediately and broadly shared. As researchers, funding agencies, and policy makers become aware of the opportunities afforded by faster and wider sharing of research results, access policies are evolving accordingly. From policies focusing primarily on protecting this material from unauthorized users, a proliferation of policies designed to leverage the value of funding agencies' investment in research by sharing the results as widely as possible are now appearing. This paper will examine the rapid evolution of access policies, designed to create a more inclusive scholarly communications playing field, which are now appearing around the world.

KEYWORDS. Public access policies, scholarly communication, research results, open repositories

THE ISSUE

Funders, particularly government agencies, invest resources in support of research with the explicit expectation that this research will result in improvements for the good of the public. They anticipate that the results of research will spur the advancement of scientific discovery and innovation, help to provide stimulus for the economy, and that this, taken in turn, will contribute to the improvement of the lives of the public.

There is a growing recognition that the communication of the results of research is an essential component of the research itself. If resources are invested in conducting an experiment, and no one ever learns of the results, what point was there in conducting the research in the first place? The dissemination of the results is a crucial part of the experiment.

Research is also, by nature, a cumulative process. It is only by sharing the results of one's work, and by inviting others to build on it that we see science advance. Accordingly, it is only through use of research findings that funding agents can obtain value from their investment in research. Broad, fast, and seamless sharing of research results helps to fuel the advancement of science, and to ensure that the funding agents' investment in that research is maximized.

Up until fairly recently, funding agents could be reasonably sure that their investment in research was being maximized by the dissemination of findings though traditional channels—namely, printed, subscription-based journals. It would have been quite impractical, inefficient, and expensive for them to consider taking on the task of broader dissemination of the results themselves. But as we know, the Internet changed everything and now presents us with an important new opportunity to bring information to new readers at virtually no marginal cost—making expanded access to research, in the view of many agencies, not only feasible, but necessary.

Today, even it if is available electronically, the research paid for by public institutions is, in too many cases, still simply not widely available. Users face obstacles in trying to access all the research they need at the time they need it. Funding agents, particularly government sponsored funding agents, recognize that this works against their interest, as well as the public interest, because this research is not being fully used and applied.

We are now beginning to see the emergence of policies that are designed to eliminate access barriers in order to allow research results to not only be more easily accessed but, just as critically, more easily shared and used.

The recognition that new opportunities existed for better dissemination of this information was an important milestone, and was not, in fact, initially articulated in any government policy, but rather in series of "declarations" that were signed by thousands of individuals, institutions, and funding bodies around the world, pointing out the need for a more open system of access to research.

These declarations included the Budapest Open Access Initiative,[1] the Berlin Declaration on Open Access to Knowledge in the Sciences and Humanities,[2] and more recently the Salvador Declaration on Open Access.[3]

Since the issuance of these declarations, concerns about access to research results have been echoed and reinforced by a wide variety of civil-society institutions and now, in ever-growing number, by political bodies at national and international levels. Increasingly, these calls for enhanced access policies are rooted in the direct recognition that increased access to and use of research not only advances science, but also drives innovation and promotes economic competitiveness.

The call for greater access has been growing in volume and momentum, and one notable characteristic is that it has been growing from both the grassroots level and percolating upward, as well as from the government agency level, and trickling downward.

AN ISSUE FOR THE PUBLIC

Grassroots public support for the concept of public access to the results of publicly funded research, not surprisingly, runs deep. This was illustrated by the findings of a Harris Poll released in May 2006,[4] which explored the public's attitude toward accessing the results of scientific research on the Internet. Eight out of ten adults polled believe that if tax dollars pay for scientific research, people should have access to results of the research on the Internet.

Additionally, the poll showed that six out of ten (62 percent) believe that if these research results are easily available (for free and online), it will help speed up the discovery of potential cures for diseases.

As the results of the Harris Poll illustrate, the call for public access to publicly funded research results addresses the general public's rising interest in self-education on health matters and the need to see the results of their investment.

It's critical to remember that the general public is comprised of teachers, doctors, nurses and other health practitioners, small business owners, and others who have both a vested interest in this material and a demonstrated need for it. Patient advocacy groups have been particularly active in highlighting the barriers that they face in trying to get access. Sharon Terry, President of the Genetic Alliance and mother of two children with a rare genetic disease called PXE, has described the problem in personal terms:

> When we went to try to find [information on PXE], we discovered that it was very hard to get. We lived in the Boston area at the time and were lucky to be able to go to one of the best medical libraries in the world. We went to the Harvard University library and found that we had to pay $25 to get in the door, which we understood because it's a private university. So we paid the $25, but after about ten trips to the library we decided we couldn't afford to continue that way.[5]

AN ISSUE FOR THE LIBRARY

Even if Ms. Terry could afford to continue to pay the entry fee required to begin to look for the information she required, there is no guarantee that she would be able to do so—at least not without incurring additional fees.

The largest single purchaser of scientific research results (in the form of journals) is the academic and research library community. Yet no library can say that they can provide access to all of the research that may be of interest to its users. In fact, not even the wealthiest private research institution in the United States can afford access to 100 percent of the peer-reviewed research that it wishes to provide to its users, and for thousands of public and private colleges, universities, and research centers in the United States, the situation is far worse. This severely hampers the library's ability to fulfill an essential part of it's mission—providing patrons with access to information that they need in order to successfully carry out their research agendas.

AN ISSUE FOR THE UNIVERSITY

This, in turn, has a negative effect on the parent institution of the library, particularly when that institution is a university or college. Awareness of this issue, and of the new opportunities presented by networked digital technology, is beginning to bring down these longstanding barriers, and has been building in the higher education community as well.

Over the past year the provosts and presidents of more than 130 leading U.S. universities and colleges have expressed their support for a policy that would ensure broad public access to the results of research funded by U.S. government agencies.

In one such statement, published as an open letter in the publication *Inside Higher Education*, the provosts of twenty-five leading U.S.

universities encouraged the community to look for a new way of disseminating research findings. They wrote:

> The broad dissemination of the results of scholarly inquiry and discourse is essential for higher education to fulfill its long-standing commitment to the advancement and conveyance of knowledge. Indeed, it is mission critical.... In keeping with this mission, we agree with the basic premise that enabling the broadest possible access to new ideas resulting from government-funded research promotes progress, economic growth, and public welfare. Furthermore, we know that, when combined with public policy such as [The Federal Research Public Access Act—FRPAA] proposes, the Internet and digital technology are powerful tools for removing access barriers and enabling new and creative uses of the results of research.[6]

This letter was particularly notable in part because it articulated the importance of the opportunities that access to this subset of research can create, and highlighting the importance of new and innovative *uses* for these research results that the academic and research community is currently unable to sufficiently leverage:

"Widespread public dissemination levels the economic playing field for researchers outside of well-funded universities and research centers and creates more opportunities for innovation. Ease of access and discovery also encourages use by scholars outside traditional disciplinary communities, thus encouraging imaginative and productive scholarly convergence."[7]

The provosts concluded that a policy enabling broad public access to research results "is good for education, and good for research."

AN ISSUE FOR RESEARCHERS

There are strong signs that the research community would agree with that conclusion. In an unprecedented show of support for greater access to publicly funded research results, more than 20,000 individual researchers and research institutions signed a petition presented to the European Commission in February of 2006 calling for the Commission to guarantee public access to publicly funded research results. The researchers signed a statement that underscored their collective belief that, as researchers, their mission of disseminating knowledge was "only half complete if the information is not made widely and readily available to society."[8]

These recent, strong statements by leaders in both the higher education community and the research community are reflective of a deepening understanding of the sea change in how science is conducted that has been underway for the past several decades. The vast majority of scientific research is data driven, interdisciplinary, and takes place almost entirely in cyberspace. Capturing the digital results of publicly funded research and ensuring that they are made broadly accessible in interoperable repositories further leverages the public's investment in research, by creating a unique series of resources that can be used in new and innovative ways—providing direct benefit to researchers and to the public as a whole.

Additionally, a growing body of evidence illustrates another benefit that is increasingly motivating researchers to press for greater public access to research results. Over the past five years, studies[9,10] have shown that when scientific research is *accessed* more frequently, it has *greater impact* on subsequent research.

This is important on two fronts. First, on an individual level, impact is an important criterion in funding, promotion and tenure decisions. Second, on a much larger, community level, these finding demonstrate how public access, by eliminating use barriers, can expand the application of research to further advances.

A MARKET ISSUE

Because of the amount of money involved—in the United States alone, the Federal Government invests tens of billions of dollars in research annually[11]—the mechanisms for disseminating these results, and the businesses that carry out this dissemination are of keen interest to market analysts. And dissemination of this information is big business—according to Outsell, a market research company that covers the STM publishing industry, the STM market totaled nearly nineteen billion dollars in revenue in 2006.

Publishing industry analysts at various firms have been tracking the industry for years, but signs that the market was ripe for change began emerging in earnest in 2004. For example, analysts as Credit Suisse First Boston wrote about the imperative for change in this 2004 report, which pointedly noted:

> We would expect governments (and taxpayers) to examine the fact that they are essentially funding the same purchase three times:

governments and taxpayers fund most academic research, pay the salaries of the academics who undertake the peer review process and fund the libraries that buy the output, without receiving a penny in exchange from the publishers for producing and reviewing the content.... We do not see this as sustainable in the long term, given pressure on university and government budgets.[12]

It's Now a Policy Issue

And indeed, governments (and taxpayers) have, in fact, begun to examine exactly this phenomenon. Governments, acting both on their own (such as Australia[13]) or working in concert (such as within the OECD[14]), have commissioned a number of reports targeted at analyzing the state of the market for dissemination of research results. As these reports have been completed and the resulting recommendations made public, some striking themes have emerged.

For example, in a 2005 report on scientific publishing, the International Organization for Economic Cooperation and Development (OECD) examined the current workings of the scholarly publishing marketplace, and concluded: "Governments would boost innovation and get a better return on their investment in publicly funded research by making research findings more widely available." And that by doing so, they would "maximize social returns on public investments."[15]

Shortly thereafter, in 2006, the European Commission published its report on the findings of their own extensive independent study of the economic and technical evolution of the scientific publishing market. The authors of the report note:

"Scientific publication ensures that research results are made known, which is a precondition for further research and for turning this knowledge into innovative products and services ... [G]iven the scarcity of public money to provide access to scientific publications, there is a strong interest in seeing that Europe has an effective and functioning system that speedily delivers results to a wide audience."[16]

The report included a series of recommendations for future action, and its number one recommendation was that research-funding agencies should "guarantee public access to publicly-funded research results shortly after publication." This recommendation, which became the focus of the European Union-wide petition discussed earlier, is expected to be taken up for debate by the European Parliament later this year.

In the United States, in an open letter to members Congress, twenty-five Nobel Laureates expressed their strong support for action to be taken to ensure that the results of publicly funded science are made broadly accessible to the public, saying:

"Science is the measure of the human race's progress. As scientists and taxpayers too, we therefore object to barriers that hinder, delay or block the spread of scientific knowledge supported by federal tax dollars—including our own works."[17]

WORLDWIDE MOMENTUM TOWARDS ACCESS POLICIES

The theme of "public access to research as soon as possible after publication in a peer-reviewed journal" has become a cornerstone in policies that are currently under consideration worldwide in ever-increasing numbers. In the United States, this language appears in such prominent examples as the National Institutes of Health's Public Access Policy,[18] along with the proposed Federal Research Public Access Act of 2006,[19] which spans eleven of the largest agencies that provide funding for scientific research.

Worldwide, policies that essentially have this language at their core have emerged from such geo-politically diverse agencies as the Research Councils United Kingdom (RCUK)[20] and the Ukrainian Parliament[21]; The Canadian Institutes of Health Research[22] and the South African Academy of Sciences[23]; The French National Research Center[24] and The German Research Foundation[25]; and these policies are now in various states of play: from formally adopted (leading off with five of the eight UK Research councils adopting mandatory public access policies) to pending action within reasonably short time frames (the CIHR, for example, is expected to announce a formal policy before the end of 2007).

Common Themes in Policies

Commonalities in these policies emerging from widely geographically diverse locations are not limited to simply calling for public access to the results of publicly-funded research as quickly as possible. The policies also share many common drivers, which have been articulated in various publications and forums, and include a number of crucial points.

Perhaps most important among these is the explicit recognition and articulation that the dissemination of results is an inseparable, essential component of research and of the funding agent's investment in that research.

This simple, powerful belief, coupled with the understanding that new technologies present previously unobtainable opportunities for expanding the communication of research results, is the key tenet driving the creation of these new public access policies.

It is also crucial that framers of many of these policies also explicitly seem to recognize the power of these public access policies to expedite, expand, and strengthen their ability (and in fact, their national ability) to leverage their investments in scientific research. This drive for the ability to realize a markedly increased return on a collective investment in research has served as a powerful incentive. In almost all cases, supporters of these emerging policies point to the potential in allowing greater access to research results to create and provide new avenues for use of federally funded research results and to stimulate new discoveries and new innovations.

And one final commonality has also emerged in terms of drivers—these fledgling policies hold the appealing promise that they can also increase a funding agent's ability to track results of research in which they have invested—increasing both the transparency of the organization, as well as the accountability of the agent to the public.

Common Elements in Emerging Policies

It is also quite striking to note that as these policies have emerged, several elements have been consistently present in the actual structure of the policies. Almost without exception, the policies include (with slight variations, of course) these elements:

1. The policies generally require that the recipient of funds from the granting agencies deposit of copy of a final manuscript that has been accepted for publication in a peer-reviewed journal into and online repository approved/sanctioned by that granting agency.
2. The policies also generally require that repositories in which the manuscripts are deposited must be stable digital repositories that provide for free public access to the manuscript, that provide for maximum interoperability, and that also makes provisions for long-term preservation of and access to the manuscripts.
3. And finally, the policies generally stipulate that free, public availability of manuscripts must be enabled as soon as possible

after publication, with the current time period defining "as soon as possible" ranging from 0 to 12 months after publication in a peer-reviewed journal.

These consistencies in the proposed implementation of the policies underscore the consistencies of purpose in the policies that they are designed to support.

Emerging Elements in Policies

Of course, while the elements described above have remained quite stable over the past several years as these policies evolved, there are several areas where new elements, or variations of these elements, have begun to emerge. There are several areas where nuances in the basic elements have begun to crop up, which may ultimately become staples of the policies as well.

One such area is in giving a researcher more options in how to comply with a requirement for public accessibility of their research results. In a few cases (most notably in the draft CIHR policy[26]), proposals have been included that would give funding recipients the option of depositing their accepted manuscript in an openly accessible repository, with an embargo period in place, **or**, alternatively, to publish their manuscript in an Open Access journal with no embargo period in place.

As policies have evolved, more flexibility has been slowly introduced in terms of the location and type of repository sanctioned by the policy. For example, when the NIH public access policy was introduced, it required deposit in a single, centralized database, PubMed Central (PMC). While the current NIH policy continues to require deposit in PMC, the agency has also begin to implement mirror sites with reciprocal deposit arrangements in countries outside of the United States, ensuring researchers that their material will have the archival protection that co-location in geographically diverse databases provides, as well as the additional benefit of links to material funded by other agencies whose research outputs are complementary to those of the NIH.

Perhaps the most striking kind of arrangement appears in the proposed Federal Research Public Access Act, which requires that manuscripts be "preserved in a stable digital repository maintained by that agency or in another suitable repository that permits free public access, interoperability, and long-term preservation."[27]

This language allows for a wide variety of possible solutions to be conceived, ranging from each agency constructing its own database solution, to agencies collaborating in various configurations to achieve economies of scale and other operating efficiencies, and even to the possibility that agencies might collaborate with organizations outside of the federal government, in public-private partnerships with institutions who share similar values or missions. This flexible approach can enable individual communities to implement solutions that best respond to their differing cultural and financial circumstances, norms, and requirements.

Finally, several of the organizational bodies that have public access policies currently under consideration have expanded their discussions of the need for broader public access to cover research outputs *in addition* to peer-reviewed journal articles. In both Canada and Australia, for example, policy discussions have included research data as well.

The inclusion of data in a handful of these policies highlights the likelihood that policy-level interest in leveraging significant investments in research will only continue to grow. As the benefits of faster and broader access and use of primary research literature are realized, it is quite likely that pressure to see similar results by unlocking the underlying data will intensify as well. In the context of the policies currently under consideration, it is unclear at this time whether, given the complexities inherent in dealing with raw data, it will be able to be successfully considered as one component in a larger public access policy or if it will indeed require a separate policy designed to specifically accommodate its own unique traits.

Regardless of how these variations ultimately play out, a clear trend has become evident—public access policies are surfacing in ever-increasing numbers, and with striking similarities, from around the world. The emergence of these policies is indicative of new and deepening collective understanding of opportunities presented by the digital research environment to more fully exploit results of research collectively funded by the public.

NOTES

1. Budapest Open Access Initiative, February 14, 2002, http://www.soros.org/openaccess/read.shtml.
2. Berlin Declaration on Open Access to Knowledge in the Sciences and Humanities, October 22, 2003, http://oa.mpg.de/openaccess-berlin/berlindeclaration.html.

3. Salvador Declaration on Open Access, September 23, 2005, http://www.icml9.org/channel.php?lang=en&channel=91&content=439.

4. "Most Americans Back Online Access To Federally Funded Research," Wall Street Journal Online, http://online.wsj.com/article_email/SB114893698047965609-1MyQjAxMDE2NDM4MTkzMzE2Wj.html.

5. Sharon Terry, SPARC Forum, January 15, 2005, http://www.arl.org/sparc/meetings/ala05mw/Sharon_Terry.htm.

6. Open Letter, http://insidehighered.com/news/2006/07/28/provosts.

7. Ibid.

8. EU Petition for Guaranteed Access to Publicly-Funded Research Results, http://www.ec-petition.eu/.

9. Lawrence, Steve (2001). "Free online availability substantially increases a paper's impact." *Nature* 411, no. 6837, 521.

10. Eysenbach G. Citation Advantage of Open Access Articles. PLoS Biol. 2006;4(5) p. e157. http://dx.doi.org/10.1371/journal.pbio.

11. Federal Research Public Access Act of 2006, Sen. John Cornyn, http://cornyn.senate.gov/index.asp?f=record&lid=1&rid=237171.

12. Credit Suisse First Boston, Sector Review: Scientific, Technical, and Medical Publishing, April 6, 2004.

13. Department of Education, Science and Training Report, 2006, http://www.dest.gov.au/sectors/research_sector/policies_issues_reviews/key_issues/australian_research_information_infrastructure_committee.

14. International Organization for Economic Cooperation and Development, Report on scientific publishing, 2005, http://www.oecd.org/document/55/0,2340,en_2649_34487_35397879_1_1_1_1,00.html.

15. Ibid.

16. Study on the Economic and technological Evolution of Scholarly Publishing, ec.europa.eu/research/science-society/pdf/scientific-publication-study_en.pdf.

17. "Open letter to the U.S. Congress Signed by 25 Nobel Prize Winners," August 26, 2004, http://www.fas.org/sgp/news/2004/08/nobel082604.pdf.

18. NIH Public Access Policy.

19. Federal Research Public Access Act of 2006.

20. Research Councils United Kingdom (RCUK), *Open Access Policy*, http://www.rcuk.ac.uk/access/default.htm.

21. and the Ukrainian Parliament.

22. The Canadian Institutes of Health Research, *Draft Public Access Policy*, http://www.cihr-irsc.gc.ca/e/33925.html.

23. The South African Academy of Sciences, *Policy for Measurement of Research Outputs*, http://www.education.gov.za/dynamic/imgshow.aspx?id=2120.

24. The French National Research Center, *Open Access Policy*, http://www.irisa.fr/activity/new/007/irisaopenarchive006?set_language=en.

25. The German Research Foundation, *Open Access Policy*, http://www.dfg.de/en/news/information_science_research/other_news/info_wissenschaft_04_06.html.

26. CIHR, *Draft Public Access Policy*.

27. Federal Research Public Access Act of 2006.

Funes and the Search Engine

Frank Menchaca

ABSTRACT. This article considers the challenges and opportunities publishers and libraries face in redefining themselves in the digital age. Migrating resources from print to electronic format represents only one aspect of this redefinition. Both entities must make their resources findable via the search engines that are increasingly the first and last stop in research by students and by faculty. And findability itself amounts to more than making library collections work seamlessly with the Internet; it also requires a more user-centered approach to product development, design, and communication/marketing. Drawing on a wide variety of culture reference points, this article addresses learning, research, and strategic planning.

KEYWORDS. Information architecture, libraries, user focus, literature, digital learning, cognition, digital research, library collections

I wear a red-handed stare whenever I am caught combining fact with fiction. The reason I do not call these two by their other names—truth and lies—is that those carry a moral authority, the promise and threat to vindicate or condemn, and my purpose here is to illustrate, not legislate. Nevertheless, I admit a sense of guilt at being found out mixing the hard, verifiable data of the outside world with imagination.

Yet I do this all the time, for the simple reason that fiction—the unreal, the imagined—knows more and tells more, if not about the extensible world, then certainly about our experience in that world.

So, indulge me a moment as I come to the topic of libraries and digital resources in the twenty-first century via the path of a short story. I will meander; but you may enjoy the diversion.

The character named in the story's title, "Funes, el memorioso" (Funes the Memorious One) by Jorge Luis Borges, is, in the style of idiot savants, also a kind of super processing chip. After a fall in early childhood, Funes is left with the ability of total recall, a memory that instantly records for immediate retrieval, everything in minutest detail.

This scene presents the story's narrator, punctuating an interview with Funes in a dim room, near the end of this extraordinary character's life, with a description of his peculiar gift and burden:

> With one quick look, you and I perceive three wineglasses on a table; Funes perceived every grape that had been pressed into the wine and all the stalks and tendrils of its vineyard. He knew the forms of the clouds in the southern sky on the morning of April 20, 1882, and he could compare them in his memory with the veins in the marbled binding of a book he had seen only once, or with the feathers of spray lifted by an oar on the Río Negro on the eve of the battle of Quebracho.... He told me that in 1886 he had invented a numbering system original with himself, and that within a very few days he had passed the twenty-four thousand mark. He had not written it down, since anything he thought, even once, remained ineradicably with him. His original motivation, I think, was his irritation that... thirty-three Uruguayan patriots should require two figures and three words rather than a single figure, a single word. He then applied this mad principle to other numbers. Instead of seven thousand thirteen (7013), he would say, for instance, "Maximo Perez"; instead of seven thousand fourteen (7014), "the railroad"; other numbers were "Luis Melian Lafinur," "Olimar," "sulfur," "clubs," "the whale," "gas," "a stewpot," "Napoleon," "Augustin de Vedia." Instead of five hundred (500), he said "nine." Every word had a particular figure attached to it, a sort of marker; the later ones were extremely complicated.... I tried to explain to Funes that his rhapsody of unconnected words was exactly the opposite of a number system.[1]

Imagine a cataloger run amok, or perhaps in the throes of an extremely high fever, reading your card catalog at random by number and title. There you have Funes.

This character's unusual affliction allows him to instantaneously capture and store every piece of information, yet prevents him from putting any of it to use. He recalls each detail of an entire day; and, so precise are his recollections, it takes him an entire day to do it. The result is simple repetition. Funes cannot forget. And because he cannot forget he cannot choose—include some things and leave others out. He cannot sort and if he cannot sort, he cannot fuse similar or disparate things. He cannot abstract. Funes can hold the whole world in his mind; but he cannot think.

And in this, he is like a library, or a search engine, without librarians—or, I should say, librarians who are able to perceive a new role for themselves.

As I wrote these words, I conducted an experiment. I launched a Google search on the date on which I was writing: February 16, 2007, exposing myself as a hopeless procrastinator, for this was three days prior to the conference's paper submission deadline. My search retrieved 954,000,000 records in one sixtieth of a second. The time was 6:26 a.m. and though I had, so to speak, the entire day at my fingertips, I was in the absurd position of likely needing thirty-six hours to just to get through Web sites pertaining to the present twenty-four. I was a Funes in the making.

I think this is so with many of us. Digital resources are so ubiquitous we get lost in them. Access to seemingly everything at once is convenient but the convenience is exhausting. If we, as publishers and libraries, do not find a means of, to use Dean Lee's conference organizing principle, bridging the gap, connecting users to not all digital content, but to the right digital content, we risk leaving the users of our products, the patrons of our libraries, to become, on their own, a new generation of Funeses; able to capture and store data in astonishing quantities, but underserved in the skill of productively utilizing those data to create ideas.

To build the bridge, we must first understand what habits of utility those users have. How do they live? I'll borrow Hamlet's principle of finding out my direction by indirection, and hopefully arrive at a view of the users we serve through the work of DJ Spooky That Subliminal Kid, a.k.a. Paul D. Miller. Allow me to give you the opportunity to "pick up on what I'm puttin' down," and call your attention to one of his creations.

The credits on Spooky's CD, which, by the way, accompanies a provocative and articulate manifesto on the cultural role of the DJ, "Rhythm Science," tell us that the track mixes beats by Oval, a German techno outfit, Japanese electronica by Yoshihiro Hanno, and an archival recording of James Joyce reading "Anna Livia Plurabelle," from *Finnegan's Wake*. An interesting experiment? Gimmick? Or is this the sound of learning a twenty-first century literature student makes in your university?

Turn to Miller's manifesto where he at first defines his "shareware persona," DJ Spooky, as a kind of Funes for the digital age:

> The idiot as processing device, slave to the moment, outside of time because there is for him only the moment of thought. No past, no present, no future. The idiot is a zombie, a character straight out of *Thriller,* one of Michael Jackson's chorus line of decaying bodies moving into y'all's neighborhoods.[2]

Less post-modern. More post-frat party. In any case, there is more to this persona than meets the eye. In a less cinematic moment, Miller defines DJ Spooky as "a living engagement with ultra media-saturated youth culture."[3] Like his contemporaries—the students who use my products and your libraries—this "living engagement" is not just a passive receptor of information overload, he or she is an orchestrator of data, existing in a multimedia present tense while processing, editing, fusing, and thinking. The late teens and early twenty-somethings who pass through your library turnstiles trailing tunes from iPods, like clouds of second-hand digital smoke, may indeed be learning—sorting disparate data, facts, and opinion, becoming, if you will, anti-Funeses—in a different way, one which we, as publishers and libraries, must understand if we hope to advance it, if we hope to stay relevant. To quote a source closer to home, from Elizabeth J. Wood, Rush Miller, and Amy Knapp in *Beyond Survival: Managing Academic Libraries in Transition*:

> Instead of the library professional being determined to direct...[the] reference interview through a linear progression—from general information in encyclopedias and dictionaries to exploration of increasingly esoteric sources—exploration of the topic can start with a tangential aspect and backtrack through specific and general treatments of the topic at a pace comfortable to the researcher before ultimately arriving at the desired balanced treatment.[4]

The Internet has made more available than ever before a wider variety of information, in an array of media, and the avatars by which students enter this data world may be sonic, e-textual, perhaps even via the anime series Avatar. How should this change the way we do our jobs?

Answer that question with this question: What do users want to know? The University of California Berkeley's 2006 study, "Use and Users of Digital Resources: A Focus on Undergraduate Education in the Humanities and Social Sciences"—one of the few, to my knowledge, comprehensive surveys of just what resources are used and for what purpose—exposes our shocking lack of typology for both people and products:

> We know very little about how digital resources, such as those produced at research universities, are actually being used by the different tiers of higher education institutions both in the U.S. and abroad. There is an implicit assumption that faculty at a variety of institutions import digital content to enhance their undergraduate teaching. We simply do not know, however, if such importation occurs on a measurable scale. And if it doesn't, why not?[5]

More often than not, the Berkeley research found, students use what they can find and professors use what they are accustomed to. Libraries pay thousands of dollars a year for digital resources they carefully select and review. In the rapidly reconfiguring world of educational publishing, publishers invest millions in products and their CFOs dangle return on investment like the sword of Damocles over the product developer's pate. If getting it right means making and buying the right products, then we have huge incentives to do so. How is it that faculty and student use of quality digital resources remains so chancy?

Images. News. Online reference sources. Video. Maps. After literally hundreds of user interviews, focus groups, an H-Net survey, and numerous other data gathering activities, the Berkeley study found, among faculty, these are the most consulted digital resources (Figure 1).

In today's higher education equation—which might be named a quest for the holy grade—faulty preferences drive student behavior. What do these results say about both groups? Images reign supreme; no surprises there: today's college sophomore was born in 1987. His eyes opened to the debut episode of *The Simpsons,* Bob Barker's first appearance on *The New Price Is Right* since deciding to go gray, and the seemingly fiery curtain call for Dallas's Pam Ewing, as her sports car spun out of control and exploded in the show's season finale.

Professors reach today's students through the image, if not before, then probably simultaneously with, the word. The Berkeley study indicates this occurs over a range of subjects (Figure 2).

How much the student decides to use these depends on how two things: how careful the professor is in choosing them and, I would propose, how large a role the librarian has played in that decision-making chain. Fast forward from Pam Ewing's burning wreck to 2007. Our sophomore is a

FIGURE 1. Types of Digital Resources Used by Faculty. Reproduced from Harley et al. (2006) with permission. Available at http://digitalresourcestudy.berkeley.edu/.

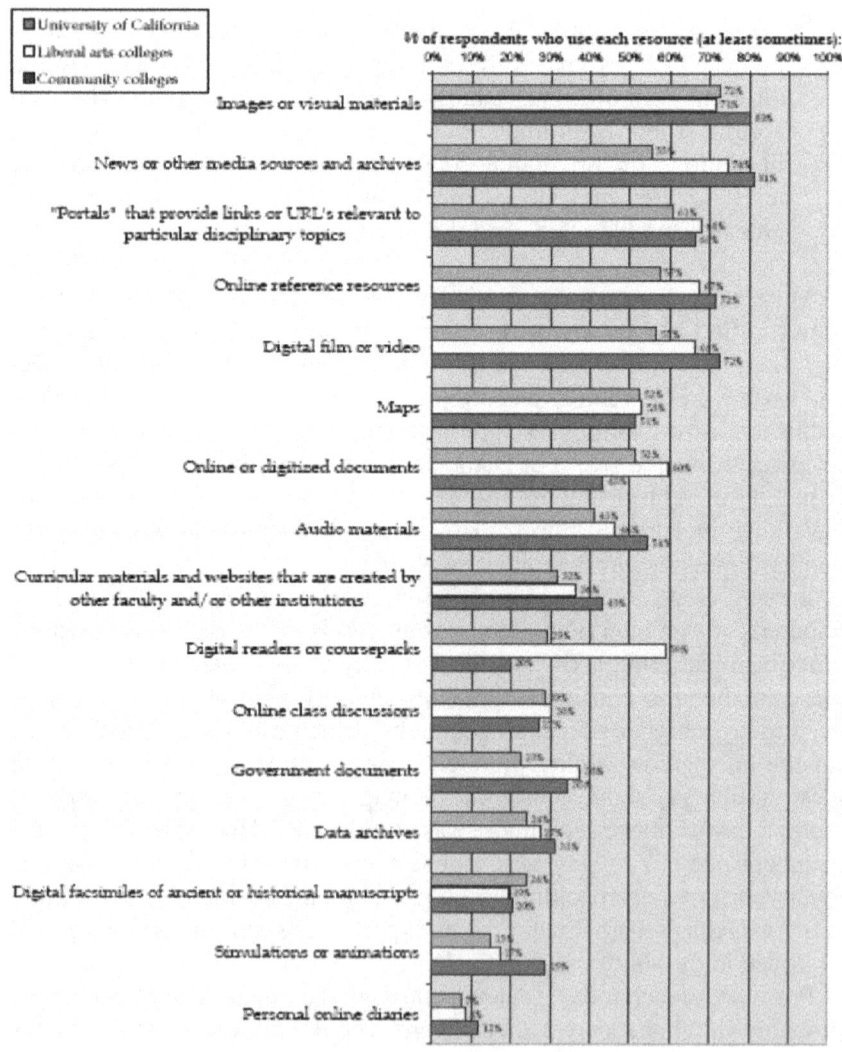

University of Oklahoma English literature major. He is fulfilling an elective in the Literary and Cultural Studies requirement, with a Group II course in "Drama of the Restoration and the 18th Century." It is the eve of a 10-page paper deadline. A visually-functioning creature, he searches "18th Century

FIGURE 2. Types of Digital Resources Used by Faculty. Reproduced from Harley et al. (2006) with permission. Available at http://digitalresourcestudy.berkeley.edu/.

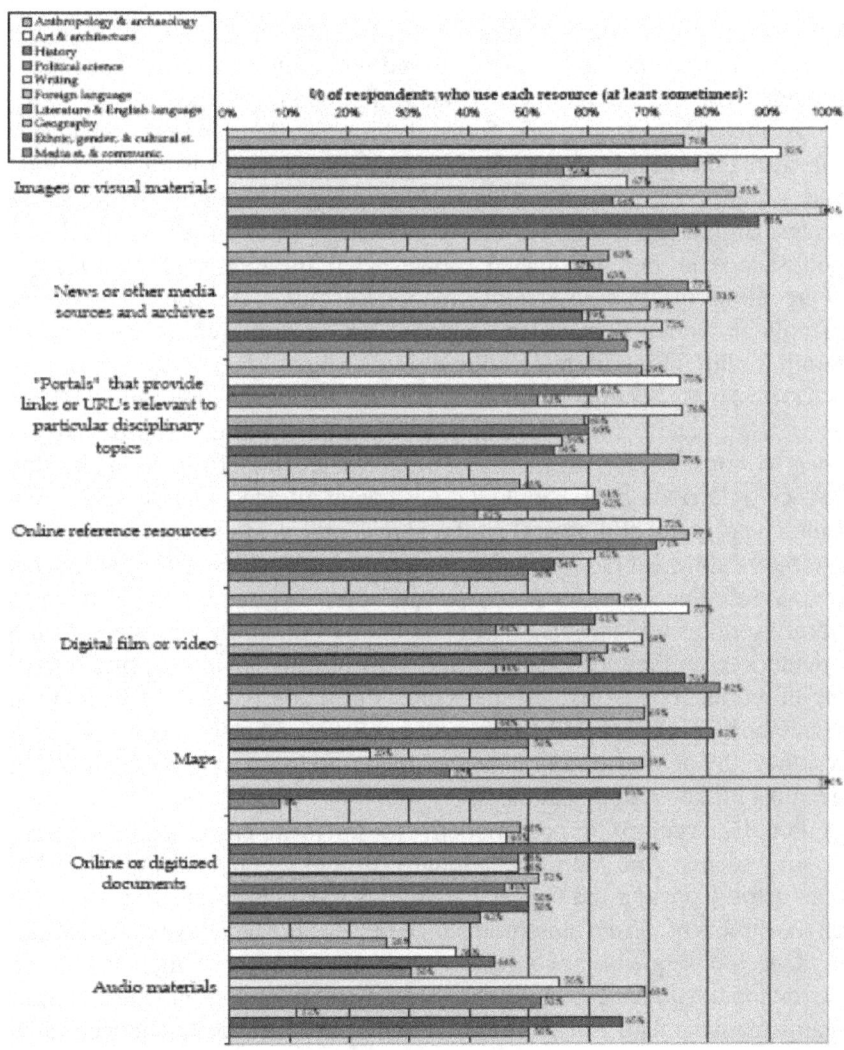

Drama" on Google Images and retrieves scanned covers from books on the topic from Amazon and Cambridge University Press, visuals from courses in Canada and California, a Hamilton College press release. On YouTube the same search produces a four minute Korean drama, two trailers for the movie "Perfume," and a clip called "Riding the Viral Dream," which describes itself as the first film short to be rated NC-17 by the MPAA rating board where no actor in the film appears nude or engages in a live sexual act. Hmm. It's 2:00 a.m. The paper is due in ten hours. My own palms flood with sweat in sympathy to his rising desperation. Squeeze the margins. Find some Cliff's notes. An old school, low-grade reference tool provides a simple path to the answer. Well, hope for the best.

Oklahoma's proactive and forward-thinking librarians no doubt have foreseen this disaster and habituated their students to using the OPAC and library research collections, where they will find, among other things, Eighteenth Century Collections Online. Before I, as that product's publisher, can feel vindicated, however, I am reminded by OCLC's "Perceptions of Libraries and Information Resources" that only 8–9 percent of college students across the country are "extremely" or even "very" familiar with online library resources.[6]

Google must become your OPAC and my product catalog. And students as well as faculty must be taught to distinguish your resources as the ones to consult first. Numerous initiatives are underway to make this so—Google Book Search and OCLC's recent alliance, Gale's Access My Library program, and others. At the University of Michigan and Drexel's Internet Public Library initiative, graduate information science students review reference questions from around the world and connect them to library sources for answers. When freshmen troop into your library during orientation, do they learn how to find your resources? Introducing library digital collections as part of the search infoscape is only the beginning. "Findability" is key and librarians and publishers need to foreground those resources by demonstrating why they matter to users' objectives. In short, we must all know our customers.

iPod. E-learning. Our post-modern customers are pre-vowel everything, or so it seems. And their educational priorities are not necessarily what ours were. Consider the Center for Studies in Higher Education's finding on the effects of virtual classrooms, like those at the University of Phoenix:

"One consequence of greater cross-border e-learning may be a narrowing of subject concentration. Seeking to maximize income and meet mainstream demand, much cross-border higher education has concentrated on strongly career-oriented provision (notably business, IT, healthcare, and education.)"[7]

E-learning is pan-national and in ten years, maybe sooner, your library and my business may be serving business majors in Oaxaca. This hardly augurs the end for either of our institutions or for our shared love of the liberal education, the program that broadly trains minds. In the second decade of the last century Henry Adams predicted that the Virgin and the Dynamo—religion and industry—would rule the era. He was pretty close to correct for the twentieth century and it appears that he had a head start on the twenty-first, even if ours will be the age of religion and technology: the Virgin and the Microchip, the Prophet and the Processor. Big ideas—religion, progress—still occupy the minds of our students, above and beyond their desire to cash a paycheck. They need us to serve both types of needs and our success depends on how much we can change our priorities to follow their priorities.

This raises social, economic, and educational issues. The transformation that the student into a client carries many consequences. For example, the notion of age (accumulation of experience) disappears from the conversation if you look at students no longer for what they are (not too much general culture, certainly less than the librarian, teacher, publisher!), pupils, but as buyers/clients—a status where their "life experience" (or lack thereof) matters less; a status that makes them inevitably right: we must listen to what they want, because if we don't, they will not buy. With this in mind, following "their priorities" takes on a dimension that certainly puts educators in an uneasy position in relation to their own authority.

Wood, Miller, and Knapp, as well as many others, refer to the paradigm shift user focus has initiated in libraries. To illustrate how dramatic this transformation in perspective has been, let me read you the rules for using Northwestern University Library (Figure 3).[8]

Posted in 1887, these regulations, only slightly more punitive than the state of Texas, could have easily survived in most libraries into 1997. In 2007, it is not hard to imagine some librarians waxing nostalgic for them. Certainly, we publishers pine for the time they represent: When librarians were not competing with search engines for granting access to information, it meant publishers had no such worries.

The ubiquity of information—and, yes, at least some is quality, authoritative information that has little to do with what I make and what you select—means that users might do just fine without libraries and publishers. Everything hinges on the conditional: *might*. In *Ambient Findability: What We Find Changes Who We Become*, Peter Morville charts the quality of a decision (read: *idea* or *thinking*, an end product of data gathering and sorting) against volume of information (Figure 4).[9]

An increase in decision quality mirrors an increase in information volume, but only to a point. Saturation ensues; information overflows,

FIGURE 3. Library Rules. Reproduced with permission of the Northwestern University Library. http://www.library.northwestern.edu/archives/exhibits/architecture/image.php?iid=315.

LIBRARY RULES.

I. The Card-catalogue, Poole's Index, and other guides are placed at the service of those using the Library; when these aids prove insufficient, help may be sought from the Librarian or his assistants.

II. Books of reference, periodicals, and other works belonging to important sets, or reserved for any reason by the Library Committee, may not be taken from the Library. Other books may be drawn for two weeks.

III. No student may keep from the Library more than two volumes at one time. For every volume retained beyond the limit of the rule or the time specified by notice, a fine of two cents a day will be charged.

IV. For marking or writing in any book, periodical, or newspaper, or for any other injury, a fine will be imposed according to the extent of the damage.

V. Conversation and all conduct tending to disturb those using the Library are prohibited.

VI. No one may go behind the reading-tables without the Librarian's permission. Permission will ordinarily not be given to more than four at a time.

VII. No one will be entitled to the use of the Library while any fine against him remains unpaid.

Northwestern University, Nov. 1. 1887.

and soon, very soon, the researcher goes from wading, to treading water, to inundation. Our freedom of choice of information, posits Morville, becomes, ultimately a prison: a state of paralysis in which, because seemingly all options are available, all are equal. And if all are equal, which are right? Or to repeat a quote attributed to Groucho Marx: "If everybody's somebody, then nobody's anybody." Writes Morville:

> Because our trust in authority has eroded, we must find our own solutions. We select our sources. We choose our news. But since we're swimming in information, our decision quality is poor. So, how do we stop from drowning? We fall back on instinct. We retreat from data. We drop pull and endure push. We pay attention only to

FIGURE 4. Quality of a Decision vs. Volume of Information. Reproduced from Morville (2005) with permission.

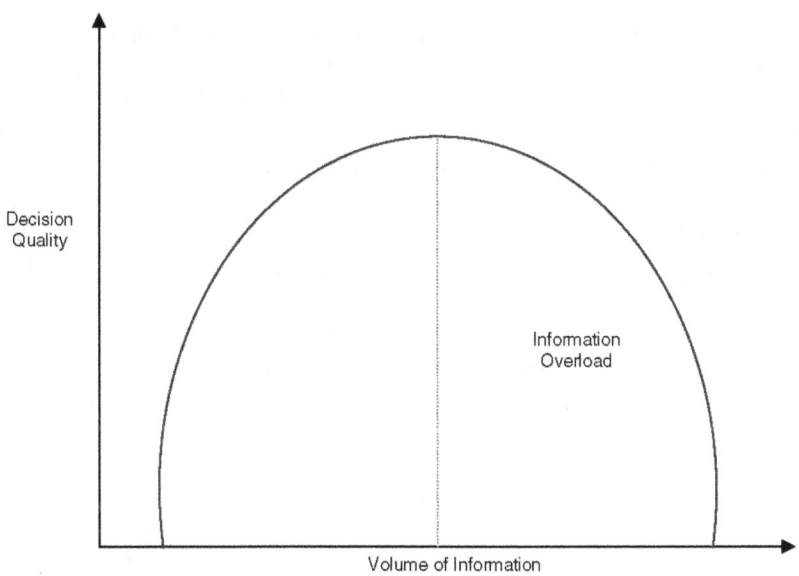

the messages that find us. And when we do, we skim. A keyword or two into Google, a few good hits, and we're done. We satisfice with reckless abandon, waffling back and forth between too much information and not enough.[10]

We have the ability—indeed the obligation—to become trusted authorities, arbiters of the best resources and good enough. Not intrinsic in our status, our educational background, how smart we are, nor how much we've read, this authority is conferred upon us by our users if and only if we demonstrate our understanding of what decisions they wish to make and put all of our resources at the service of those decisions.

So, let me finish by sharing the prescriptions I've written to myself, and perhaps you may find them useful.

Pledge to serve your end user before serving your institution. That is the only way you will make the goals of the latter the goals of the former.

Know what your user wants. To accomplish that, you must go out to the faculty and convince them that you have the ability to help them shine by putting them in touch with better resources than they are used to. In a world of measurable outcomes, their soaring course enrollments will make them stars. Remember, their goals will drive student needs. Fulfilling those needs and wants will be glory reflected back to you.

Think like Toyota. Plan your business not in quarters, nor in years, but in decades. See your user as ascending a scaffold of information literacy that begins in pre-school and rises over two decades. Academics, start planning your library strategies in K–12 and public libraries. They are not in our audience today. If we don't include them, we are missing an opportunity to teach users the difference between library and non-library resources. If they know that, they will know what to do when they arrive at university, without being told.

There are others; but those are enough. Difficult? Certainly. Paradigm breaking? Maybe.

The alternative is a world of shelf on shelf of printed books, page on page of search-engine results, under-qualified, overabundant, and to our calls not just for information, but also understanding, essentially mute—the world, in short, of Funes.

NOTES

1. Borges, Jorge Luis, "Funes, His Memory," in *Collected Fictions*, Andrew Hurley, trans. (New York: Viking, 1998), 135–136.

2. Miller, Paul D., *Rhythm Science* (Cambridge, MA: MIT Press/Mediaworks Pamphlet, 2004), 9.

3. Ibid., 12.

4. Wood, Elizabeth J., Rush Miller, Amy Knapp, *Beyond Survival: Managing Academic Libraries in Transition* (Westport, CT: Libraries Unlimited, 2007), 8.

5. Harley, Diane et al, "Use and Users of Digital Resources: A Focus on Undergraduate Education in the Humanities and Social Sciences," (Report, April 5, 2006, Center for Studies in Higher Education), http://cshe.berkeley.edu/research/digitalresourcestudy/.

6. "Perceptions of Libraries and Information Resources: A Report to the OCLC Membership," 2005: Question 1305.

7. Quoted in Harley et al, section 2–3.

8. University Archives, Northwestern Architecture Web page, Northwestern University Library, http://www.library.northwestern.edu/archives/exhibits/architecture.

9. Morville, Peter. "Inspired Decisions. *Ambient Findability: What We Find Changes Who We Become*. (Sebastapol, CA: O'Reilly Media, 2005), 165.

10. Ibid., 166.

BIBLIOGRAPHY

Harley, Diane et al. "Use and Users of Digital Resources: A Focus on Undergraduate Education in the Humanities and Social Sciences." Berkeley, CA: Center for Studies in Higher Education: 5 April 2006. http://digitalresourcestudy.berkeley.edu/.

Morville, Peter. *Ambient Findability*. Sebastapol, CA: O'Reilly, 2005.

—. *Information Architecture for the World Wide Web*. 3rd edition, CA: O'Reilly, 2006.

Miller, Paul D. *Rhythm Science*. Cambridge, MA: MIT Press/Mediaworks Pamphlet, 2004.

—. "Perceptions of Libraries and Information Resources: A Report to the OCLC Membership." Dublin, OH: OCLC, 2005.

Sterling, Bruce, and Lorraine Wild. *Shaping Things*. MIT Press/Mediaworks Pamphlet, 2005.

Tenopir, Carol. "Use and Users of Electronic Library Resources: An Overview and Analysis of Recent Research Studies." Washington, DC: Council on Library and Information Resources, August 2003. http://www.clir.org/.

Wood, Elizabeth J., Rush Miller, and Amy Knapp. *Beyond Survival: Managing Academic Libraries in Transition*. Westport, CT: Libraries Unlimited, 2007.

Index

abandonment, internalizing concept of planned 7, 19-20
access
  home or work, access from 51
  password access 36-7
  perpetual or post-cancellation access 36-7
  Portico's electronic archiving service 36-7
  repurposing access tools 7, 17-18
  science research results, policies and practices on 95-106
  sources of revenue 6
  special collections 6
  verification access 36-7
  web-based usage surveys 51
access to science research results, policies and practices on 95-106
  collaboration 105
  common themes 102-4
  declarations 96-7
  emerging elements in policies 104-5
  enhanced access policies 97
  entry fees 98
  European Commission report, recommendations in 101
  Federal Research Public Access Act 2006, proposal for 102, 104
  funding agents 96, 103
  grassroots support 97
  libraries, effect on 98
  market issue 100-2
  National Institute of Health (NIH) Public Access Policy 102, 104
  open access, declarations on 97
  patient advocacy groups 97-8
  reports 101
  repositories, use of 104
  researchers, views of 99-100
  subsequent research, impact on 100
  universities, effect on 98-9
  worldwide momentum 102-5
administrators, leadership role of university 67
Agriculture Network Information Center – Western Rangelands 28-9
Arid Lands Information Center 27

121

Arizona *see* University of
  Arizona
ARL *see* Association for
  Research Libraries (ARL)
assessment
  digital content, assessment of
    value and impact of 41-57
  human resources 21
  performance and assessment
    measures, developing new
    7-8, 18-19
  promotion and tenure,
    evaluation of scholarship
    for 63
  skills assessments 21
Association for Research
  Libraries (ARL)
  cooperation and collaboration 10
  digital content, assessment of
    value and impact of 43-6
  DigiQUAL+ 50-1, 52
  E-Metrics 44-6
  LibQUAL+ 50-2
  New Measures Initiative 19
  performance and assessment
    measures, developing
    new 19
  preservation 32-3
  Scholar's Portal Project 11
  sources of revenue, creating
    new 20
  StatsQUAL™ 50-5
  Supplementary Statistics 45
atlases 28
audit or certification procedures
  or organizations 35

benchmarking 18
Bisbee Deportation of 1917
  exhibit 28

blogs, posting on student 14-15
Books of the Southwest 29
bottled water 78-9
budget *see* funding

castles and monasteries, building
  libraries in 71
catalogs
  repurposing 7, 17-18
  University of Arizona
    'Unbundling the Catalog'
    project 17-18
Centre for Creative Photography
  Educator's Guides 26
Centre for Creative Photography
  Exposure Project 26
Centre for Research Libraries
  (CRL) 8
certification or adult procedures
  or organizations 35
change
  cooperation and collaboration 8-9
  economics 3-30
  expenditure, changes in library
    61-2
  faculty behaviour, changes in
    62-3
  space transformation 86
  user behaviour, changes in 61-2
CIC (Committee on Institutional
  Cooperation) libraries 61, 63-7
'circle of service' model 86, 89-
  90, 91, 93
classes, services used in 14
classrooms, libraries as extension
  of 16
collaboration *see* cooperation
  and collaboration
collections and collection
  building

access 6, 105
castles and monasteries,
    building libraries in 71
consortia or collaborations,
    membership of 10-11
cooperation and collaboration 9
data sets 15
decisions 49
development 9, 49, 71-4
digital content, assessment of
    value and impact of 48-9
economics 5-7, 15-18
funding 7, 15-16
Internet 72
legacy collections 7, 16
licensing 72
looting and force, collecting
    by 71
management practices 48-9
network as library 72-3, 82
new collection analysis tools 15
partnerships 5, 6, 10-12
print collections 6
printing press, development of
    the 71
projects 9
sources of revenue 6
special collections 6, 28, 93
Special Collections Online
    Exhibits (University of
    Arizona) 28
University of Arizona Libraries 12
University of Tennessee
    Libraries' Commons,
    development process for 93
user requests 15
web-based usage surveys 51-2
Colorado State University,
    RAPID interlibrary loan
    service 10

Committee on Institutional
    Cooperation (CIC) libraries
    61, 63-7
commons see University of
    Tennessee Libraries'
    Commons,
    development process for
communications see scholarly
    communications
Community College of Vermont,
    embedded librarian program
    at 14
complexity of electronic
    resources 33, 34
Connecticut University
    Networked Services Team 49
consortia or collaborations,
    membership of 10-11
content see digital content,
    assessment of value and
    impact of
cooperation and collaboration 7-9
    Association for Research
        Libraries (ARL) 10
    Centre for Research Libraries
        (CRL) 8
    change 8-9
    CIC (Committee on Institutional
        Cooperation) libraries 61,
        63-7
    collection development projects 9
    cross-campus initiatives 12
    distinguished, cooperation and
        collaboration 8-9
    economics 12
    E-Metrics 10
    Google digitalization project 11
    interdependence 8-9
    interlibrary loans 9, 10
    LibQUAL + 10

Online Computer Library
  Center (OCLC) 9
Portico's electronic archiving
  service 37
preservation 34
Project SAILS (Standardized
  Assessment of Information
  Literacy Skills) 10
publishers 37
RAPID interlibrary loan
  service, Colorado State
  University 10
replication, reduction in 9
resource sharing 8
Scholar's Portal Project (ARL) 11

space transformation 85-6
storage facilities, sharing 8
University of Tennessee
  Libraries' Commons,
  development process for
  88-9
cost-benefit analyses 47-9
Council on Library and
  Information Resources (CLIR)
  reports 5, 34
course management systems 14

decision-making
  development collection
    decisions 49
  digital content, assessment of
    value and impact of 49
  impact of information on 79
  quality of decisions 115-17
  search engines 115-17
definition of information 77-8
demographic data 51, 52
desktop, providing all services to
  the 7, 14-15

blogs, posting on student 14-15
classes, services used in 14
Community College of
  Vermont, embedded
  librarian program at 14
course management systems 14
economics 7, 14-15
interlibrary loan requests 14
reference services 14
RSS feeds, subject-specific
  acquisition updates to 14-15
DigiQUAL 19, 50-1, 52
digital content, assessment of
  value and impact of 41-57 *see
  also* web-based usage surveys
Association for Research
  Libraries (ARL) 43-6
collection management
  practices 48-9
cost-benefit analyses 47-9
development collection
  decisions 49
electronic journals 46-9
E-Metrics 44-6
gateways, development of
  library 47
guidelines 45-6
IMS Digital Repositories
  Framework 47
International Coalition of
  Library Consortia
  (ICOLC) 45
International Organization for
  Standardisation (ISO) 45
Joint Information Systems
  Committee Information
  Architecture Environment
  (JISC IE) 46-7
management practices,
  improved collections 47-9

National Information Standards Organization (NISO) 45-6
'New Measures' initiatives 43-4
OhioLINK (Ohio Library and Information Network) 48-9
Ontario Council of University Libraries (OCUL) 48-9
Penn Library Data Farm (University of Pennsylvania) 46
print collections, assessment of use of 41-3, 48-9
Project COUNTER (Counting Online Usage of NeTworked Electronic Resources) 45-6
Project SAILS (Standardized Assessment of Information Literacy Skills) 44
standards 45-6
Supplementary Statistics (ARL Libraries) 45
SUSHI (Standardizes Usage Statistics Harvesting Initiative) 46
unit costs 47-9
University of Connecticut Networked Services Team 49
usage data 42-3
vendor supplied data and transaction based usage 45-7
Digital Millennium Copyright Act (DMCA) 13
digital outreach projects 12, 25-30
digitalization
  Google digitalization project 11
  mass digitization, guiding principles and support for 66, 67

University of Tennessee Libraries' Commons, development process for 87

economics, academic libraries and 3-30
  campus, focusing on needs of 7, 12-13
  catalogs and access tools, repurposing 7, 17-18
  change 3-30
  collections, collection building and collection budget, rethinking 7, 15-16
  cooperation and collaboration 7-9, 10-12
  costs, reducing 4-5
  Council on Library and Information Resources (CLIR) report 5
  cross-campus initiatives 12
  desktop, proving all services to the 7, 14-15
  digital format, collections in 6, 7
  Finding Information in a New Landscape (FINL) project 5
  forecasting 3-30
  funding, reduction in 4
  human resources, changes in utilization of 7, 20-1
  institutional repository building 11
  legacy collections 7, 16
  locally what must be done locally, only do 7, 9-12
  management of campus knowledge and information 6, 13
  national information policy, role of librarians in 6

national systems for maintaining and preserving information in all formats 6
online journals, creation of new 12
partnerships 5, 6, 12
performance and assessment measures, developing new 7-8, 18-19
physical learning environment, provision of 6
planned abandonment, internalizing concept of 7, 19-20
print collections 6
production of knowledge 5-6
productivity, increasing 4-5
Project on the Future of Higher Education 4-5
'push out' philosophy, need for adoption of 5-7
redesigning spaces as learning spaces 7, 16-17
sources of revenue, creating new 7, 20
special collections and unique resources, digital access to 6
stimulation of research and knowledge 5
technology 3-30
transformation and transition 4-21
University of Arizona Libraries 5, 12-13, 25-30
University Teaching Center 12-13
virtual learning environment, provision of 6
'what we do' concept 12
workflow design 5
e-learning 114-15
electronic journals
Association for Research Libraries (ARL) 32-3
complexity 33
Council on Library and Information Resources (CLIR) report *E-Journal Archiving Metes and Bounds: a Survey of the Landscape* 34
digital content, assessment of value and impact of 46-9
economics 12
Journal of Evolutionary Ecology Research 12
Journal of Insect Science 30
new journals, creation of 12
Portico's electronic archiving service 35-9
preservation 32-3, 34
University of Arizona 12
web-based usage surveys 51-2
Electronic Theses and Dissertations (ETD) 29-30
embedded librarian program at Community College of Vermont 14
E-Metrics 10, 19, 44-6
end of information 74-6
ending services 19-20
entry fees 98
European Commission report on access to research results 101
excess of information 79-80, 108-9, 115-17
expenditure, changes in library 61-2

EZproxy 54

faculty behaviour, changes
 in 62-3
Federal Research Public Access
 Act 2006, proposal for 102,
 104
fees 37, 98
findability 114
Finding Information in a New
 Landscape (FINL) project 5
fragility of electronic
 resources 33
funding
 access to science research
  results, policies and
  practices on 96, 103
 collections, collection building
  and collection budgets 7
 Portico's electronic archiving
  service 38
 publishers 38
 reductions 4
 sources of revenue, creating
  new 7, 20
 University of Tennessee
  Libraries' Commons,
  development process for
  90, 91

gap-analysis tools 50
gateways, development of
 liberal 47
Google
 digitalization project 11
 library project 76
 search engine, as 109, 114
GPO (Government Printing
 Office) Digital Repository 30
graduate services 93

GROW (Geotechnical, Rock &
 Water) Digital Library 27

human resources
 changes in utilization 7, 20-1
 economics 7, 20-1
 librarians, role of 21
 professionals who are not
  librarians, using 21
 skills assessments 21
 University of Tennessee
  Libraries' Commons,
  development process for 90

IMS Digital Repositories
 Framework 47
information convergence 70-1, 76
information monopoly 73-4, 75
information overload 79-80
information ubiquity 70-1, 74,
 76, 78-82, 115
institutional repository building
 11, 65-6, 67
instructional software,
 availability of 13
intelligence analysts 79
interlibrary loans
 cooperation and collaboration
  9, 10
 desktop, proving all services to
  the 14
 RAPID interlibrary loan service,
  Colorado State University 10
International Coalition of Library
 Consortia (ICOLC) 45
International Organization for
 Standardisation (ISO) 45
Internet
 collections and collection
  building 72

Mosaic 74
search engines 107-19
Iraq, information overload on 79-80

Joint Information Systems Committee Information Architecture Environment (JISC IE) 46-7
Journal of Evolutionary Ecology Research 12
Journal of Insect Science 30
journals *see* electronic journals

legacy collections 7, 16
Legacy Technical Reports 30
LibQual+ 10, 19, 50-2
librarians and information professions, effect of technology on 6, 21, 75-83
library collection development *see* collections and collection building
library space *see* space
licensing 32, 72
Little Cowpunching newspaper 28
locally what must be done locally, only do 7, 9-12
  Association for Research Libraries (ARL) Scholar's Portal Project 11
  consortia or collaborations, membership of 10-11
  deals, negotiation of 10
  economics 7, 9-12
  outsourcing 9-11
  partnerships, creating collaborative 10, 11
  preservation 10

looting and force, collecting by 71

marketing 78-9, 90
MINES (Measuring the Impact of Networked Electronic Services) 19, 50-1, 52-5
monasteries and castles, building libraries in 71
monopoly of information 73-4, 75
Mosaic 74

national information policy, role of librarians in 6
National Information Standards Organization (NISO) 45-6
National Institute of Health (NIH) Public Access Policy 102, 104
national systems for maintaining and preserving information in all formats 6
Networked Digital Library of Theses and Dissertations 29
networks
  Agriculture Network Information Center – Western Rangelands 28-9
  MINES (Measuring the Impact of Networked Electronic Services) 19
  network as library 72-3, 82
  Networked Digital Library of Theses and Dissertations 29
  OhioLINK (Ohio Library and Information Network) 48-9
  preservation 34-5
  Project COUNTER (Counting

Online Usage of
   NeTworked Electronic
Resources) 45-6
University of Connecticut
   Networked Services Team
   49
'New Measures' initiatives 19,
   43-4, 50-1
noise-to-signal ratio 80-1

Office of Information Technology
   (OIT) 86, 88-90, 92
OhioLINK (Ohio Library and
   Information Network) 48-9
Online Computer Library Center
   (OCLC) 9
Online@UT 88
Ontario Council of University
   Libraries (OCUL) 48-9, 52-3
open access 64, 66, 67, 74, 97
outreach projects 12, 25-30
outsourcing 9-11

partnerships 5, 6, 10-12
password access 36-7
patient advocacy groups 97-8
performance and assessment
   measures, developing new 7-
   8, 18-19
   ACRL standards 19
   Association for Research
      Libraries (ARL) New
      Measures Initiative 19
   benchmarking 18
   DigiQUAL 19
   E-Metrics 19
   LibQUAL + 19
   MINES (Measuring the Impact
      of Networked Electronic
      Services) 19

Project SAILS 19
perpetual or post-cancellation
   access 36-7
photography 26
physical learning environment,
   provision of 6
planned abandonment,
   internalizing concept of
   7, 19-20
policies see access to science
   research results, policies and
   practices on
Portico's electronic archiving
   service for journals 35-9
   assessing the archive 36-7
   community reactions 38-9
   cooperation of publishers 37
   fees 37
   financial support 38
   libraries, role of 37
   licences, termination of 36-7
   participation, criteria for 37
   password access 36-7
   perpetual or post-cancellation
      access 36-7
   publishers
      cooperation 37
      funding 38
   sustaining the archive 38
   trigger events 36
   'Urgent Action' statement 37
   verification access 36-7
preservation see also Portico
   (electronic archiving service)
   Association for Research
      Libraries (ARL) 32-3
   audit or certification procedures
      or organizations 35
   Center for Research Libraries
      (CRL) and RLG Programs

Trustworthy Repositories Audit & Certification: Criteria and Checklist (United States) 35
changing landscape 32-5
complexity of electronic resources 33, 34
cooperation 34
Council on Library and Information Resources (CLIR) report *E-Journal Archiving Metes and Bounds: a Survey of the Landscape* 34
Digital Curation Centre (UK) and Digital Preservation Europe's toolkit *Digital Repository Audit Method Based on Risk Assessment* 35
diverse approaches 34
electronic journals 32-3, 34
fragility of electronic resources 33
infrastructure 33
licensed electronic materials 32-3
locally what must be done locally, only do
multiple agents 34-5
national systems for maintaining and preserving information in all formats 6
networks 34-5
recommendations 34
Research Libraries Group – National Archives and Records Administration Task Force on Digital Repository Certification 35
response to challenges 33-5
scale of challenge 34-5
'Urgent Action' statement 33
Penn Library Data Farm (University of Pennsylvania) 46
print collections
 assessment of use 41-3, 48-9
 economics 6
printing press, development of the 71
productivity, increasing 4-5
professionals who are not librarians, using 21
Project COUNTER (Counting Online Usage of NeTworked Electronic Resources) 45-6
Project on the Future of Higher Education 4-5
Project SAILS (Standardized Assessment of Information Literacy Skills) 10, 19, 44
public relations 78-9, 90
Publishing Agreements, Joint Statement with CIC University Faculty Governance Leaders on 64-5
'push out' philosophy, need for adoption of 5-7

Rangeland Monitoring in Western Uplands 27
RAPID interlibrary loan service, Colorado State University 10
reference services 14
replication, reduction in 9
repositories
 access to science research results, policies and practices on 105

institutional repository building 11, 65-6, 67
research *see also* access to science research results, policies and practices on economics 5
Journal of Evolutionary Ecology Research 12
Research Libraries Group – National Archives and Records Administration Task Force on Digital Repository Certification 35
scholarly communications 59-68
stimulation of research 5
University of Tennessee Libraries' Commons, development process for 93
web-based usage surveys 53
Resumé Builder 13
RSS feeds, subject-specific acquisition updates to 14-15

sampling plans 50
Scholar's Portal Project (ARL) 11
science research results *see* access to science research results, policies and practices on scholarly communications 59-68
administrators, leadership role of university 67
changes in user behaviour 61-2
CIC (Committee on Institutional Cooperation) libraries 61, 63-7
electronic format, publication in 62-3

evaluation of scholarship for promotion and tenure 63
expenditure, changes in library 61-2
faculty behaviour, changes in 62-3
institutional repositories, establishment and support of 65-6, 67
mass digitization, guiding principles and support for 66, 67
Open Access Initiatives 64, 66, 67
Publishing Agreements, Joint Statement with CIC University Faculty Governance Leaders on 64-5
standards 66
university presses 67
search engines 107-19
e-learning 114-15
findability 114
Google 109, 114
habits of users 109-13, 117-18
information overload 108-9, 115-17
quality of decision 115-17
resources used, types of 110-13, 117-18
rules for using libraries 115, 116
ubiquity of information 115
University of California Berkeley 2006 study 110-11
software, availability of instructional 13
sources of revenue 7, 20

Association of Research Libraries (ARL) 20
business plans 20
coffee shops and food, selling 20
creating new sources 7, 20
fundraising and grant programs 20
special collections, scanning, building rights and reproduction services from 20
students and student fees 20
space
 'circle of service' model 93
 classrooms, libraries as extension of 16
 collaboration 85-6
 computers, installing 16
 economics 7, 16-17
 learning spaces, redesigning library spaces as 7, 16-17
 Office of Information Technology (OIT) 86
 redesigning spaces as learning spaces 7, 16-17
 scenario for change 86
 social/cultural space 91-2
 transformation 85-94
 University of Tennessee Libraries' Commons, development process for 85-93
special collections
 access 6
 source of revenue, as 6
 Special Collections Online Exhibits (University of Arizona) 28
 University of Tennessee Libraries' Commons, development process for 93
standards
 ACRL standards 19
 digital content, assessment of value and impact of 45-6
 International Organization for Standardisation (ISO) 45
 National Information Standards Organization (NISO) 45-6
 performance and assessment measures, developing new 19
 scholarly communications 66
 SUSHI (Standardizes Usage Statistics Harvesting Initiative) 46
Starbucks Café 88, 91-2
StatsQUAL™ 50-5
storage facilities, sharing 8
Supplementary Statistics. Association for Research Libraries (ARL) 45
Support for English Composition Courses 28
SUSHI (Standardizes Usage Statistics Harvesting Initiative) 46

teachers, digital instructional materials for 13
telephone services 13
Tennessee *see* University of Tennessee Libraries' Commons, development process for too much information 79-80, 108-9, 115-17
transformation and transition 4-21, 85-94

Tree of Life (TOL) 27-8

ubiquity of information 70-1, 74, 76, 78-82, 115
'Unbundling the Catalog' project (University of Arizona) 17-18
unique resources, digital access to 6
unit costs 47-9
University of Arizona 5, 12-13
  Agriculture Network Information Center – Western Rangelands 28-9
  Arid Lands Information Center 27
  Arizona Archives Online (AAO) 29
  Arizona Electronic Atlas 26
  Arizona-Sonora Desert Museum (ASDM) Online 26
  Arizona-Sonora Documents Online 29
  Bisbee Deportation of 1917 exhibit 28
  Books of the Southwest 29
  Centre for Creative Photography Educator's Guides 26
  Centre for Creative Photography Exposure Project 26
  digital collection building projects 12
  Digital Millennium Copyright Act (DMCA) 13
  digital outreach projects 12, 25-30
  economics 5, 12-13, 25-30
  electronic journals 12
  Electronic Theses and Dissertations (ETD) 29-30
  Finding Information in a New Landscape (FINL) project 5
  GPO Digital Repository 30
  GROW (Geotechnical, Rock & Water) Digital Library 27
  instructional software, availability of 13
  Journal of Evolutionary Ecology Research 12
  Journal of Insect Science 30
  Legacy Technical Reports 30
  Little Cowpunching newspaper 28
  Networked Digital Library of Theses and Dissertations 29
  Rangeland Monitoring in Western Uplands 27
  Resumé Builder 13
  Special Collections Online Exhibits 28
  Support for English Composition Courses 28
  teachers, digital instructional materials for 13
  telephone services 13
  Tree of Life (TOL) 27-8
  UA Libraries Special Collections 28
  'Unbundling the Catalog' project 17-18
  Western Waters Digital Library 30
University of California Berkeley 2006 study on digital resources 110-111
University of Connecticut Networked Services Team 49

University of Pennsylvania Penn
    Library Data Farm 46
University of San Diego (UCSD)
    54-5
University of Tennessee
    Libraries' Commons,
    development process for
  'circle of service' model 86,
    89-90, 91, 93
  collaborations 88-9
  Digital Library Center 93
  Digital Media Service 88, 89-90
  Digital Production Unit 87
  digitalization 87
  expansion 91
  funding 90, 91
  gate count, increase in 90-1
  graduate services and
    faculty 93
  Greer Room 92
  guiding principles 89
  Hodges Library 87-8
  human resources 90
  Media Services and Studio area
    92-3
  Office of Information
    Technology (OIT) 86, 88-
    90, 92
  Online@UT 88
  phase two 91-2
  phase three 92-3
  presentations 90
  public relations subgroup 90
  research and inspiring
    spaces 93
  Reserve Book Room 88
  Services and Space Study
    Group 87-8
  social/cultural space, commons
    as 91-2

  space transformation 85-93
  Special Collections 93
  Starbucks Café 88, 91-2
  steering committee 88-9, 92-3
  success, indicators of 90-1
  VolPrint 88
  Welcome Center 92
university presses 67
'Urgent Action' statement 33, 37
users
  changes in behaviour 61-2
  collections, collection building
    and collection budgets 15
  digital content, assessment of
    value and impact of 42-3
  print collections, assessment of
    use of 41-3, 48-9
  Project COUNTER (Counting
    Online Usage of
    NeTworked Electronic
    Resources) 45-6
  search engines, habits of users
    and 109-13, 117-18
  SUSHI (Standardizes Usage
    Statistics Harvesting
    Initiative) 46
  vendor supplied data and
    transaction based
    usage 45-7
  web-based usage surveys 49-55
  website enabling users to find
    information on their own
    51-2

vendor supplied data and
    transaction based usage 45-7
verification access 36-7
Vermont, embedded librarian
    program at Community
    College of 14

virtual learning environment,
 provision of 6
VolPrint 88

water 78-9
web-based usage surveys 49-55
 access from home or office as
  most desired core item 51
 coursework 53
 demographic data 51, 52
 DigiQUAL + 50-1, 52
 EZproxy 54
 gap-analysis tools 50
 inclusiveness 50
 interception of users 50
 LibQUAL + 50-2
 MINES for Libraries™ 50-1,
  52-5
 'New Measures' toolkit 50-1
 Ontario Council of University
  Libraries (OCUL) 52-3
 research 53
 sampling plans 50
 StatsQUAL™ 50-5
 University of San Diego
  (UCSD) 54-5
 website enabling users to find
  information on their own
  51-2
 work, print and electronic
  journal collections required
  for 51-2
Western Waters Digital Library
 30
'what we do' concept 12
workflow design 5

For Product Safety Concerns and Information please contact our EU representative GPSR@taylorandfrancis.com
Taylor & Francis Verlag GmbH, Kaufingerstraße 24, 80331 München, Germany

www.ingramcontent.com/pod-product-compliance
Lightning Source LLC
Chambersburg PA
CBHW052025290426
44112CB00014B/2385